## BOOKS BY ROGER A. MORSE

*The Complete Guide to Beekeeping*

*Bees and Beekeeping*

*Comb Honey Production*

Editor, *Honey Bee Pests, Predators and Diseases*

*Rearing Queen Honey Bees*

*Making Mead*

English Editor, *Honey Bee Brood Diseases* by Henrik Hansen

*A Year in the Beeyard*

*Beeswax* with W. L. Coggshall

*The Illustrated Encyclopedia of Beekeeping* with Ted Hooper

*ABC and XYZ of Bee Culture* with Kim Flottum

# ROGER A. MORSE

THE NEW

## Complete Guide to

# BEEKEEPING

The Countryman Press
Woodstock · Vermont

**Library of Congress Cataloging-in-Publication Data**

Morse, Roger A.
  The new complete guide to beekeeping  /  Robert A. Morse.
    p.   cm.
    Includes index.
  ISBN 0–88150–315–0
    1.   Bee culture.   I.   Title.
  SF523.M76  1994                                          94–3657
  631'.1--dc20                                                CIP

Cover design by Julie Gray
Text design by Sally Sherman
Page composition by Design & Format
Photographs by the author unless otherwise credited

Printed in the United States of America
10 9 8 7 6 5 4 3 2 1

Published by The Countryman Press, Inc.
P.O. Box 175 · Woodstock · Vermont  05091

# CONTENTS

---

⬡8⬡

---

---

⬡9⬡

---

---

⬡10⬡

---

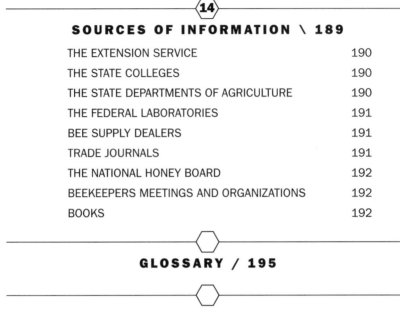

## 14

## SOURCES OF INFORMATION \ 189

## GLOSSARY / 195

## INDEX / 204

---
⬡ 1 ⬡
---

# BEES AND BEEKEEPING

THERE ARE OVER 100,000 BEEKEEPERS IN NORTH America. Of this number, only about 1,500 make their living producing honey and beeswax or regularly rent their bees for pollination. They may own from 600 to 60,000 colonies each. Another 1,500 are part-time beekeepers, who may own anywhere from 50 to several hundred colonies. The remainder, nearly 97 percent of beekeepers, are hobbyists, who keep one to fifty hives for a variety of reasons.

Many part-time and hobby beekeepers aspire to become full-time beekeepers so that they may become their own boss and work outdoors. Beekeeping, unlike many agricultural pursuits, lends itself to either slow or rapid growth. One may own any number of colonies. There comes a time at which a growing business will need a large building to house equipment, but many part-time beekeepers successfully run their operations out of a kitchen, a garage, or a small outbuilding. However, there is not as large an investment in land in beekeeping as there is in most farming operations. Honey bees gather food over an area of about four or more square miles, using both crop plants and weeds. They harvest what would otherwise be a wasted sugar supply.

Some hobbyists produce honey and beeswax that they sell from their homes or at roadside stands to supplement their income. Still others grow bees to provide themselves and their neighbors with honey. A few hobby beekeepers rent some or all of their bees to orchardists or other growers for pollination. And a small number of people keep bees to study their biology. Honey bees are adaptable animals and may be kept in a variety of hives, including glass-walled observation hives. It is possible to have an observation hive in one's office or living room as well as in a laboratory. As long as the bees have an entrance to the outdoors, they are content.

Honey bees are not domesticated animals. They do not recognize their owners as do horses, dogs, and many other animals. Although beekeepers and researchers have selected various races because they are better producers, gentler, or better pollinators, honey bees are as wild and untamed today as they ever were. We are able to keep bees and manipulate colonies because we understand bee biology and have learned how to keep them in hives designed for our convenience. Successful beekeepers apply this accumulated knowledge to assist bees in making honey.

Perhaps one of the greatest advantages of working with honey bees is that we can move colonies hundreds or even thousands of miles with no adverse effects on the bees. In one experiment, colonies were moved to a flowering pear orchard in Canada from more than five miles away. At 11 A.M. the colony entrances were opened and watched. One pollen-laden bee, having completed her foraging trip, returned to her hive 14 minutes later. In the 15th minute, six more pollen-laden bees returned to their colonies. The number of returning bees continued to increase in succeeding minutes. This remarkable ability of honey bees to reorient themselves in a new location is one factor that has made migratory beekeeping and commercial pollination possible.

## GOALS OF THIS BOOK

This book was written to teach beekeepers how to produce honey and beeswax. A beekeeper who produces as much honey as possible thoroughly understands bees, beekeeping, and bee biology. Producing a crop of honey brings into play many factors, including wintering, spring management, good queens, the importance of food to the colony, major and minor honey flows, good combs, pests and diseases, bee space, the proper equipment for beekeeping, and more. If one can manage a colony so as to produce a maximum crop of honey, then the other uses of bees, including pollination or merely observation, follow easily.

These goals are not difficult to attain. Unlike many animals, bees do not need daily attention. At certain times of the year, however, specific operations must be performed, and they must be done on time. If one is precise, it may be possible to visit an apiary only 10 to 12 times a year to maximize production.

## THE VALUE OF HONEY BEES TO OUR ECONOMY

The beekeeping picture is changing, and within the past decade we have seen many beekeepers, who once produced only honey, devoting much or all of their efforts to the production of bees for pollination. Over a million colonies are rented annually for this purpose; most of these colonies are rented twice and for use on two crops, usually in the spring. This is discussed in more detail in Chapter 10, which is devoted fully to pollination.

The lives of most flowering plants and bees are intertwined. All bees use pollen and nectar as their sole foods. The reverse is not always true, and some plants are pollinated by animals other than bees. Mammals, birds, and a great variety of insects may carry pollen from the male to the female sex organs of flowering plants. But for most plants the honey bee is the most successful pollinator. Equally, if not more important, we now have considerable knowledge of honey bee biology, which enables us to raise and transport large numbers of honey bees with ease.

## ADJUNCT BUSINESSES

There are several separate businesses within the beekeeping industry. One is the rearing of queen honey bees. Some beekeepers rear their own queens, but many grow queens for others. Queen bees in a cage with four

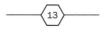

*Queen cells about to hatch are placed in small nucleus colonies such as this. The young queen flies from this small colony and mates, after which she will be captured and used to head a new colony.*

to eight attendants may be shipped through the mail from one side of the continent to the other, or from Hawaii to the mainland, with no difficulty.

Some beekeepers grow bees that they sell by the pound. One may buy packages, containing two to four pounds of bees (there are approximately 4,000 bees in a pound) and a queen, in a wire-screened box that, again, may be shipped long distances. When the package bees are received they are fed and placed in a new hive, where they usually prosper.

Other specialty businesses include packing honey, making foundation for new comb, and selling bee supplies. Some nationwide bee supply manufacturers have regional and local dealers.

## WHERE MAY BEES BE KEPT?

Food is one of the chief factors that limits where bees may be kept. A colony of bees will collect and use about 150 pounds of honey and 40 to 50 pounds of pollen for its own needs during the year. Good locations will enable a colony to make an additional 50 to 150 pounds of honey that the beekeeper may harvest.

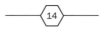

*The hairy body of this worker honey bee is well suited for accidentally carrying pollen from one flower to another. The pollen basket on the outer side of the hind leg is empty. Photo by C. Weiss.*

Cold regions, deserts, and heavily wooded areas also limit where bees may be kept, but even a few beekeepers in such cold climates as Alaska manage to winter their bees successfully by giving them special protection and food. It has been found in recent years that a large number of colonies survive in deserts in Arizona and California provided they have access to water. Nectar and pollen flows by several species of desert plants can be intense and sufficient for the needs of a few colonies.

Commercial beekeepers seek to establish apiaries in locations where there is sufficient food for 40 to 50 colonies. Keeping fewer colonies on any one site forces the beekeeper to spend too much time on the road between apiaries. Measuring the carrying capacity of an apiary site takes three to five years, and one does not expect all apiaries to be equal. Honey plants are discussed in Chapter 11.

## WHAT IS A GOOD APIARY SITE?

A good apiary site is one that is secluded, exposed to full sunlight, and close to a multitude of flowering plants; it must have good air circulation

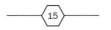

*Removing a partially filled comb of honey from a colony. The first comb removed has been set to the rear of the hive to make room to manipulate the other combs in the super. A standard comb as is illustrated here will hold five to seven pounds of honey.*

and water drainage, and a reliable source of fresh water. It is helpful to have a small building nearby in which beekeeping equipment can be kept. An access road that is usable all year round is a necessity.

The apiary site should be secluded because some people are afraid of bees, and others might vandalize the hives. While vandalism is not a serious problem, it is a temptation, especially for a youngster, to molest or even tip over a hive of bees. If an apiary site is hidden, this means that the individual bees leaving the hive must fly up and over surrounding vegetation. It also means that they cannot accidentally fly into someone walking in the vicinity. This is an interesting aspect of bee biology. Close to the hive almost any bee is quick to defend the nest. A bee disturbed in the field, on the other hand, usually flees the site of danger or interruption as soon as possible. Although an individual can be stung when not near a nest, it is a rare occurrence. Quite frequently, too, people who have been stung while walking through a field have offended a wasp, not a bee. Unfortunately, most people do not know the difference between a wasp and a bee.

We have kept an apiary of 20 to 40 colonies of bees only a few hundred yards from the active part of the Cornell University campus for many years with no difficulty. Our apiary is surrounded by a hedge about 15 feet high and about as thick. The hedge consists of evergreens, and inside the row of evergreens is a second hedge of deciduous bushes that grow to about 10 feet in height. The bees must fly up and over the hedge to forage; they are also hidden from view. We have the room to grow such a large hedge, but in more confined areas a board fence would serve the same purpose. Commercial beekeepers often place their apiaries in a woods, usually close to a good road, but hidden just enough so the colonies cannot be seen by people driving by.

An apiary should be exposed to as much sunlight as possible. Foraging bees will fly to the field earlier in the morning and will work later in the evening if their hive is warmed by the sun's rays. This is especially true in the spring and fall, critical times for honey bee colonies. A sun-warmed colony with a large force of bees to send into the field will gather more honey than a colony that is shaded and cool and has a smaller field force.

Bees maintain a brood rearing temperature of about 92° to 96°F

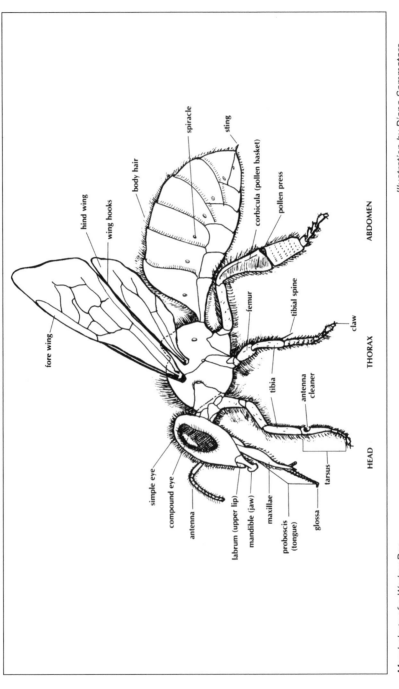

*Illustration by Diana Sammataro*

*Morphology of a Worker Bee*

(33° to 35°C). If their hives are warm and dry, fewer bees are required to produce the energy to maintain this temperature, another reason sunlight is important. The maintenance of a uniform temperature within the colony is also important in helping the colony to control certain diseases that can occur when the brood rearing temperature falls. Critical bee diseases—for example, sacbrood and European foulbrood—develop only in colonies under stress. A hive that is cool because of an improper location is one important stress factor that can be eliminated by the beekeeper.

Perhaps more important to the beginner is the question of hive temperament. Bees, or at least colonies of bees, have a temperament. On warm days, when the colony is able to maintain normal activities with little or no difficulty, the bees within the colony are much less inclined to sting. Experienced beekeepers will testify to the differences in stinging behavior between bees exposed to sun and those in shade; bees in full sunlight always have a much better temperament.

Good air circulation and water drainage are important in an apiary. It is especially important to keep colonies of honey bees dry. Colonies that are damp or have wet bottomboards have difficulty maintaining a normal brood rearing temperature. A dry hive is a healthier hive. Honey bees also give off large quantities of metabolic water when they eat honey. It is important that water be allowed to escape from the hive and not condense inside. If moisture condenses in or near the brood rearing area, it will cool the nest and make it more difficult for the bees to rear brood. ·

The best location for an apiary is on the side of a hill that slopes to the east or south and is devoid of trees in the immediate vicinity that might shade the location. While trees for a windbreak are helpful, they should not be too close to the site.

Bees collect water to dilute the honey they feed to brood and also to air-condition their nest. In the spring, water may be a critical factor for a honey bee colony. If fresh water is not available nearby, it should be provided. In remote locations a 55-gallon drum filled with water and containing some straw, leaves, or branches onto which the bees might crawl while collecting water, will provide the bees with water for up to a week or 10 days. In the home apiary, it may be possible to allow a water faucet hose to drip onto a long board from which the water may be collected by the bees.

In the northern states, beekeepers will notice that the number of bees at a watering site will increase greatly during July and August, when it becomes dry, indicating the bees' need for water. The beekeeper who locates the apiary near a source of clean water will save the bees much work.

Approximately one cell of honey and one cell of pollen are required to produce a young bee. While it is true that a bee may fly as much as eight or nine miles, if necessary, to collect pollen and nectar, research shows that colonies that gather most of their food within a half-mile radius prosper much more than those whose field force must fly further. Beekeeping is limited by the natural vegetation available to the field bees. Even the best physical location is worthless without an abundance of pollen- and nectar-producing plants.

## CITY BEEKEEPING

Honey bees are kept in Manhattan, and there was once a beekeeper's club at the Brooklyn Botanical Garden. The number of colonies that may be kept in such locations is obviously limited by the number of flowering plants. Unfortunately, too, many cities, towns, and villages have enacted ordinances that prevent beekeeping within their boundaries. However, ordinances have no effect on the number of stinging insects in an area or where they live. If one wants to eliminate honey bees from an area, one must prohibit the growing of flowering, nectar-producing plants; otherwise, swarms will find places to nest in hollow trees and buildings to take advantage of the food that is available.

Many people have kept bees successfully in cities by following some simple guidelines. These beekeepers provide water for their bees so that they will not visit birdbaths and swimming pools in the vicinity. The bees are kept behind solid fences that force the bees to fly above the heads of persons walking or working near the bees. City beekeepers seek out races of bees that are especially gentle, and they open and manipulate their colonies only under ideal weather conditions when the bees will not be aroused and sting people in the vicinity. It is especially important that a beekeeper not allow *robbing* to start because robbing bees will seek everywhere for food.

Many beekeepers will testify that giving one's neighbors a jar of honey now and then does much to calm them. The occasional lecture on the value of bees to our economy, or the joys of being a beekeeper, will also usually help. Many beekeepers offer to lecture on bees and beekeeping in grade schools, which is no doubt of value to the whole industry. School lectures accompanied by tasting sessions are invariably a success. As fewer and fewer people live on farms and keep animals, it is important to inform children about farm life and its many complications and virtues.

## BEEKEEPING EQUIPMENT

While bees have been kept for several thousand years, practical beekeeping has been possible only since 1851. In that year the Reverend L. L. Langstroth discovered the principle of *bee space* and invented the movable-frame hive. Before 1851 bees were kept in boxes or straw skeps; the bees attached their combs to the sides of the hive, and it was not possible to inspect the interior of the hive or the brood nest. Because this was true, little was known about bee diseases and bee biology; the only way honey and wax could be harvested was to kill the bees or drive them from their nest. As a result, profits per hive were low before Langstroth's discovery.

Langstroth observed that there was a fixed space of about ¼ to ⅜ inch between the combs in a natural nest. He noted that, if the spacing of the combs was not uniform, the bees would build a comb between two adjacent combs; such a comb is called a *burr comb* or *brace comb*. Langstroth found that he could take a piece of natural comb from a nest and place it in a wooden frame; if this frame was placed in a box so that there was a bee space around it, and between the frame and the box, the bees respected and used this space. The bees do not build an additional comb when the bee space is correct. Thus our present hive has a series of movable frames and combs. Because of his discoveries, Langstroth has been called the "Father of Beekeeping."

Today, several firms in the United States manufacture bee hives. Many sizes and types of hives have been built for bees over the years. Today, however, over 95 percent of the beekeeping equipment made is the 10-frame Langstroth size. Although this hive may not be perfect in every respect, bees adapt to it readily and it is a convenient size for a beekeeper to handle.

Beginners in beekeeping are advised to purchase only this standard 10-frame hive. It has a greater resale value, and its parts are interchangeable

These homemade frames with foundation are in different stages of being drawn (the cells built) by the worker bees.

with new equipment. As beekeepers gain experience, they may be tempted to try to devise a more perfect hive; unfortunately, it is probably impossible to do so. When they wish to innovate, the place to experiment is in a hive management system. No system of management is perfect; each region of

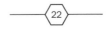

the country is slightly different, and a thorough knowledge of bee biology is required to manage a colony properly.

Three other important inventions, introduced between 1851 and 1871, followed Langstroth's discovery: comb foundation, the honey extractor, and the smoker. Of these, comb foundation is the most important. It was found that bees will accept and build a perfect comb if they are provided with a thin sheet of wax onto which six-sided cell bases are embossed. These sheets of wax are called *foundation*. While a colony of bees can build its own comb, it will not always build a straight comb. Also, there are two sizes of cells in an ordinary comb: worker cells (⅕ inch in diameter) and drone cells (¼ inch in diameter). Because drones do not collect honey, the beekeeper should be interested only in producing worker bees. The best way to control cell size is to use full sheets of a well-made foundation.

Another important invention was the honey extractor. Honey bees use a great deal of honey and energy to secrete wax and build comb. When a honeycomb is used over and over, it may remain in service for 20 to 40 years, and the bees are thus saved the effort of building new comb. An extractor is nothing more than a centrifugal-force machine. Once the wax cappings with which bees cover their full honey-storage cells are sliced off the comb, the comb is placed in the extractor, and the honey can then be spun out of the comb by centrifugal force. In this way the comb can be saved and reused many times.

The fourth and last invention important in the profitable and practical management of honey bees is the bee smoker. Using smoke in moderation helps settle bees and makes them easier to work with when you open the hive or extract frames. A smoker is nothing more than a firepot into which one may place punk (dry, rotten) wood, straw, hay, leaves, burlap, or another material that produces a heavy smoke when burned. A bellows is connected to the firepot. Pumping the bellows forces air through the fire and blows smoke out of a hole at one end.

These four major pieces of beekeeping equipment—the movable-frame hive, comb foundation, the extractor, and the smoker—were all discovered within a relatively short period of time. Since then there have been only a few minor inventions and discoveries in beekeeping equipment.

The important parts of the hive are the bottomboard, the brood nest (box or super), honey-storage supers, the innercover, and the cover. (Many beekeepers think that innercovers are not necessary.) A *queen excluder*—a series of wires 0.163 to 0.167 inch apart or a sheet of zinc with punched holes of similar width—is an important piece of equipment for most bee-keepers. A queen excluder has spaces wide enough so that workers may pass through but queens and drones cannot. If the queen excluder is placed above the brood nest, the queen is confined to that area and cannot lay eggs in the honey-storage area. An excluder need be placed on a colony only three to four weeks before the honey is to be removed. Since the development of a worker bee takes 21 days and a drone 24 days, any brood that is in the honey-storage area will emerge before the honey is removed from the hive. The use of an excluder is recommended, but not every experienced beekeeper will agree with this; some feel an excluder slows honey storage and cuts down on ventilation within the hive.

Each hive super will contain nine or 10 frames or combs. While the standard hive is designed to hold 10 frames (10 should be used when they have new foundation) most beekeepers use only nine combs in the brood nest. The slightly wider spacing makes it easier to remove combs and to inspect the brood nest; yet it also means that the bees will build more unwanted burr and brace comb. However, there should be some rotation of comb in and out of the brood nest, making sure only perfect or almost perfect worker combs are present for egg laying.

In the honey-storage area beekeepers use eight or nine combs (in the case of old combs, not foundation), evenly spaced. By using an even wider spacing for combs in which the honey is stored, bees draw out the cells, making them deeper. It is easier to uncap thicker combs of honey.

## HOMEMADE EQUIPMENT

Many commercial and amateur beekeepers make their own beekeeping equipment. There is no reason why they should not do so. In addition to saving money, it is also possible to introduce innovations the beekeeper might find useful or helpful in a management scheme.

There are two important considerations when making equipment. The first is to make sure that bee space is properly observed and built into all equipment. Second, and equally important, is that homemade equipment should be of standard size and interchangeable with all other equipment.

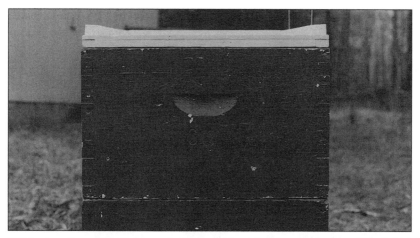

*This homemade combination cover/bottomboard is made using a large piece of ¼-inch-thick plywood. It is lightweight and works well for those who migrate with their bees. The holes are predrilled to take nails that are driven into the hive body if the colony is moved.*

As with factory-made bee equipment, it is important that all new equipment be properly nailed. Equipment that comes into contact with the ground or dampness should be protected with wood preservative. The holding power of a nail lies in its length, not its diameter or the finish coat

*Homemade beekeeping equipment, such as this cover, is satisfactory if standard dimensions are followed.*

it receives; the longer the nail the better it will hold, and it is advisable when nailing any piece of beekeeping equipment to use nails as long as the equipment will take without splitting the wood.

Some pieces of equipment that are not usually available through the bee supply houses can be made by the beekeeper. These include combination bottomboards and covers, special bee escapes, moving screens, special comb-honey supers, special bottomboards for comb honey production, and inside furniture such as free-hanging frames. (A free-hanging frame has a top bar, bottom bar, and end bars of the same width, unlike a commercially made frame with wide shoulders.)

## STANDARD DIMENSIONS

Over the years, beekeepers have probably patented more bee hives than any other piece of apiary equipment. Many people have attempted to create the perfect beehive, one that would be most acceptable to the bees and from which the greatest crop of honey could be secured. However, it is now generally agreed that there is no perfect hive, and that the management of colonies is far more important than the type of equipment in which the bees are kept.

Recently, manufacturers, most beekeepers, and state apiculturists have sought to standardize the equipment beekeepers use. While not all manufacturers make uniform equipment, there are generally agreed-upon dimensions.

## BEE HIVE PLANS

Ninety percent of the honey bees in North America are kept in boxes of a design and shape arbitrarily selected by L. L. Langstroth in 1851 and 1852. Probably 85 to 90 percent of beekeepers use Langstroth supers that hold 10 frames, but a small percentage use hive boxes that hold only eight frames. This suggests, and in fact many people have demonstrated, that bees are adaptable and can live in a variety of differently shaped boxes. However, convenience in carrying and moving bee hives is also important. Beekeepers want equipment that is interchangeable. They also want their equipment to have a reasonable resale value. These two considerations cause us to recommend that beekeepers making their own equipment use standard dimensions.

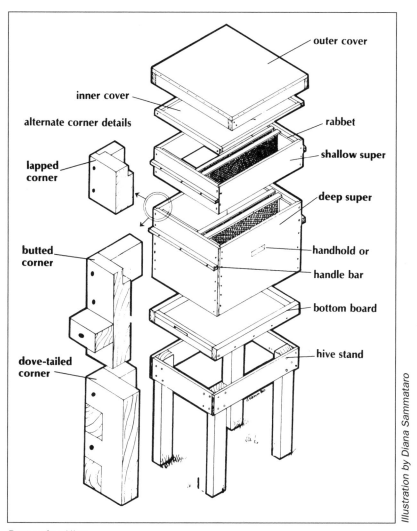

Parts of a Hive

Langstroth discovered that if a space of ¼ to ⅜ inch is left around and between the furniture in a bee hive, the bees will use this as a walking space. They will not fill this bee space with comb or *propolis,* and in this way the combs remain movable.

There are slight differences in the dimensions of beekeeping equipment made by various manufacturers. Because it is the inside dimensions of a bee hive that are important, any changes in lumber thickness must be taken into account. A variety of ½- and ¾-inch depth supers are used by beekeepers, especially for honey-storage supers. However, by far the most popular is the 6⅝-inch depth. This is the depth recommended if one does not use full-depth supers exclusively.

Many manufacturers use metal frame rests in the rabbet grooves into which the frames fit in their supers. These are not necessary and in fact may make it more difficult to clean the brown resinous substance known as propolis from the super. However, if one does not use these frame rests, the depth of the rabbet will be slightly different.

## HIVE STANDS

The hive stand is important in many parts of the United States. Very few colonies of bees rear brood throughout the year; most colonies slacken their brood rearing activities during October, November, and early December. Whenever bees are rearing brood, they attempt to maintain an interior hive temperature of about 92° to 96°F (33° to 35°C). If the bottomboard or super is damp, it is extremely difficult for the bees to maintain this temperature; additional energy will be expended and the brood may be chilled.

A hive stand that keeps the colony of bees six to eight inches off the ground and tilts slightly toward the front so that water easily drains off the colony entrance is recommended. Additionally, grass growing in front of the colony entrance slows bee flight, and a hive stand that raises the colony above at least some of the grass can help in this regard.

During the winter a properly constructed hive stand forms a dead air space immediately under two colonies pushed together for the winter pack. (See Chapter 7, "Wintering Honey Bees.")

The hive stand recommended is 48 inches long and 20 inches wide; the stand should be at least 6 inches high. The 48-inch hive stand is long enough so that the two colonies may be pulled apart during the summer, yet, when pushed together during the winter, a dead air space is created underneath if the two cross members of the hive stand are spaced 32 inches apart center to center.

Because hive stands come in contact with the ground and may rot quickly, they should be treated with either creosote or some other good wood preservative. A properly treated hive stand will last for 20 years or longer.

## MAINTENANCE OF EQUIPMENT

There are several considerations regarding the routine maintenance of bee-keeping equipment. While the physical appearance of the hives may be important to some people, there is also the question of ease of management; additionally, one should keep in mind the longevity and resale value of the equipment. At the same time, while honey bees may survive under even adverse conditions, it is important to take all steps necessary to keep the hive dry. If the hive is dry, the bees will keep it warm without further assistance.

Routine maintenance of equipment does not refer merely to painting and nailing, though these tasks are important. It is advisable to have on hand clean supers, bottomboards, innercovers, and covers, which may be used whenever the equipment in use becomes too coated with propolis or wax or needs painting or repair. As a routine practice, plan to change the supers in the brood nest area every second or third year. This is most easily done in the early spring when the colony population is at its lowest level; simply lift the frames from the old super and place them in a clean one. Doing this will make it easier to handle frames during the active season.

Spring is also an excellent time to check the quality of the combs in the brood nest. Combs with too much drone comb should be removed and replaced with good combs. Each time a worker bee is reared in a cell, its pupal case is left in the cell. While each cell is cleaned before the queen lays in it again, the old pupal case is not removed. Over a period of years, and with a successive buildup of old pupal cases, the cells become smaller. This means that the worker bees produced in these cells will be smaller. For this reason, some European beekeepers routinely replace every comb in the brood nest after four years. In the United States, combs that have been used in the brood nest for 25 or more years are common. There is no doubt that old combs produce slightly smaller bees, but we do not feel this is important; the important consideration in keeping bees is increased honey production, which depends on intelligent management. The routine maintenance of equipment should be for the purpose of making manipulations easier, thus aiding the beekeeper's management scheme.

## *Painting*

Well-painted bee hives will have a longer life. If different colored paints are used, the bees will be aided in orientation, and drifting between colonies will be reduced. Usually, beekeepers paint the top and bottom rims and outsides of supers; the inside is usually left unpainted. Placing some paint in the rabbets or frame rests will usually deter the bees from depositing too much propolis at that point for a year or two.

## DRESSING FOR THE APIARY

Female (worker) honey bees may sting. The male (drones) have no sting. Stinging is the only way honey bees can defend their nest. The alternative is for the bees to abandon their nest, and they are reluctant to do that. Most bee stings can be avoided by understanding honey bee biology. For instance, there are times of the day and weather conditions that are favorable for manipulating honey bee colonies. Also, smoke dulls a honey bee's sensory receptors, and smoked bees rarely attack.

Generally speaking, it is best to inspect a bee colony near midday when the sun is shining and there is good flight to and from the colony.

*This beekeeper inspecting a colony stands along the side of the hive, not in front of the entrance, where he might interfere with flight or invite stinging.*

Usually the older bees in a colony protect the nest, and they are, therefore, the ones most apt to sting. If most of the bees are off foraging, the beekeeper will have an easier time working in the hive. However, if there is a dearth of nectar from plants in the vicinity, even an active colony will be difficult to manage on a warm day because the foragers are in the hive, not in the field. If nectar is being brought into the colony in quantity by field bees, there are very few guard bees and very little problem with stinging bees.

It is well known that honey bees, as well as other stinging insects, are less prone to sting light-colored, smooth-finished materials. Khaki clothing is a favorite with beekeepers for this reason; white coveralls are also popular. At the same time, rough materials such as leather, suede, and felt appear to irritate bees, and they will sting these materials more readily.

The two extremes of the body, the ankles and the face, appear to attract bees. It has been suggested that the blinking of the eyes and the protrusions of nose and ears are the reasons people are often stung in the vicinity of the head. A pair of boots and a good veil will protect against stings in sensitive areas. Veils are made of black cloth or black wire over the face since it is difficult to see through any other colored material. A few beekeepers wear gloves, but this is not advised. Gloves are cumbersome; although one will receive a few more stings if gloves are not worn, the stings are infrequent and not of consequence. A gloveless beekeeper should, however, always be aware of the colony's temperament and use smoke as it is needed.

## BEE STINGS

When an individual honey bee or a honey bee nest is attacked, the bees have two choices: attack or flee. Interestingly, honey bees may flee as a group if they are disturbed too much; an individual bee disturbed in the field will almost always abscond if given the opportunity. Because the sting is the honey bee's only method of defending both itself and its nest (even though the bee, once it stings, dies), a beekeeper should expect to be stung occasionally.

Commercial beekeepers or bee inspectors, who work with bees every day, are stung frequently, often more than a hundred times a day. However, they soon build up an immunity to swelling from bee stings, and the experienced beekeeper cannot tell where he or she was stung a minute after

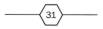

being hit by an angry bee. Being stung is part of keeping bees. The number of stings one receives may be cut to a minimum, but receiving fewer than ten or twenty stings a year makes it impossible to build up an immunity to the swelling and pain associated with stings.

It is theoretically possible—though highly improbable—for a person with one or two colonies to work through an entire season without ever being stung. To do so, however, would be to miss out on part of the action; a good beekeeper tries to avoid excessive stinging, of course, but not the occasional sting. For some it is part of the initiation into the beekeeping fraternity.

Protective clothing, the use of smoke, the time of day, the condition of the colony, and the skill of the beekeeper are all considerations in making colony manipulations. Many stings can be avoided, but to avoid all stings would be to expect too much.

There is little you can do to prevent the swelling, pain, or itching from a sting if you have not developed an immunity. A sting, if visible, should be removed. Ice applied to the area stung may slow the distribution of the venom in the system; however, the chief purpose of applying ice or a cold pack to a sting is to create a new sensation. This can be very helpful.

## SMOKERS AND SMOKE

Smoke calms bees and slows or prevents them from attacking and defending their nest. Researchers believe that smoke fouls the bees' sensory receptors, and, while guard bees may release an alarm odor when a colony is opened, the rest of the bees do not detect it.

I prefer to use the largest smoker available and to light it before entering the apiary. I use only smokers that have a protective rim of wire or some other material around the firebox so as to reduce the chances of touching it and being burned. Smokers can be dangerous. One should always light a smoker before putting on a veil to eliminate the possibility of a spark igniting the veil.

Once a smoker is lit it should be kept in an upright position. If it is placed on its side, the fire will soon die. When starting a smoker it is important to get a strong, hot fire started in the firebox or the fire will soon be extinguished.

Beekeepers use a variety of fuels in their smokers. Dried grass and

*Colonies may be examined without a veil but only under ideal weather conditions and with experience. However, it is always important to have a lit smoker nearby.*

hay are good fuels but burn so rapidly that frequent refueling is necessary. I have learned from other beekeepers that one of the best fuels is small pieces of wood taken from shop scrap. Little blocks ½ to 1 inch square will burn for a long period of time and make excellent fuel.

## OUTBUILDINGS

Before commercial beekeepers used trucks to visit their outlying apiaries, they built a small building in each location. Usually extracting was done

*Smoke is applied as the outer cover is removed and again as the innercover is lifted.*

in these locations, and the building was equipped with the necessary tools and extra hive equipment. Even today beekeepers find that buildings in out-apiaries are convenient. One usually needs a place to keep extra bottomboards, covers, innercovers, supers, etc., so they will be available when needed. Also, if a hammer and saw are on hand, equipment can be repaired.

Perhaps most important, the beekeeper may store supers or combs in an out-apiary. Although you can purchase insurance to cover the loss of drawn combs, insurance does not replace combs as rapidly as they are needed when colonies build up in the spring or when a honey flow is in progress. A beekeeper who stores combs in one location and loses them because of fire or theft may be forced out of business. Thus, commercial beekeepers generally divide their stored combs among several small buildings.

The major problem with outbuildings is that they may be vandalized. If the building is in a permanent location, a cement floor is advisable. When windows are installed, heavy shutters should be put over the outside so that vandals cannot enter the building, at least with ease. In certain parts of the country, raccoons and squirrels have been known to make their nests in outbuildings, and for this reason it is important that the buildings are secure.

## BEEKEEPING HISTORY AND LORE

The average American consumes well over 100 pounds of sugar, made from sugar cane and sugar beets, each year. However, it was only a few hundred years ago that sugar cane, which originated in the South Pacific, was introduced into Europe and North Africa. Sugar beets are of even more recent origin, having been developed in the 19th century. Thus we see that the ancient Egyptians, Greeks, and Romans did not have a ready source of sugar other than honey and a few sweet fruits. This explains why we find bees and beekeeping mentioned so many times in the Christian bible and the ancient world.

The first record of our ancestors stealing honey from a colony is a cave painting in Altamira in northern Spain that was done about 9,000 to 12,000 years ago. More recent rock-cave paintings depicting beekeeping scenes, still several thousand years old, have been found in other parts of Spain and South Africa. However, it was the Egyptians who first developed the art and science of beekeeping, probably 5,000 to 6,000 years ago. Cylindrical long hives made of dung, mud, and straw, such as are illustrated in some ancient tombs, can still be found in remote parts of Egypt today.

Interestingly, the ancient Egyptians had developed methods of dividing colonies, controlling swarming, rearing queens, and harvesting honey that were lost insofar as the Greeks and Romans were concerned. Only recently have their relatively sophisticated management schemes come to light. Honey was the most common Egyptian drug (and perhaps one of the most important). It is mentioned over 500 times in 900 of their different remedies. Since it is the sweetest of the common sugars, it was no doubt used, as it is in part today, to mask the foul taste of certain herbs and drugs. No microbes can grow in honey because of its acidity and its high osmotic pressure (see Chapter 8). It was also used successfully as a wound dressing by many ancient peoples. The body of Alexander the Great was carried back to its final resting place in Egypt in a casket filled with honey and kept in good condition in the process.

Honey bees also figured in strategic warfare, both ancient and more recent. Stories of hives of bees being catapulted onto enemy ships and in and out of castles, where they would break apart and cause bedlam, are common. Even today I have seen some beekeepers place bee hives around their homes to discourage visitors and thieves. The Roman writer, Virgil, records that he hid his silver in some bee hives during one difficult period. And I am aware of at least a few beekeepers who still use their hives as safes today.

Bees, beekeeping, and hive products continue to be important in art, both as subject material and media. The encaustic beeswax paintings from the Fayum area of Egypt that date to the first few centuries A.D. are among the world's finest artwork. Batik was originally made using beeswax. Dr. Eva Crane, in her *Archeology of Beekeeping*, discusses the art forms in more detail and includes information on beeswax modeling. She also devotes many pages of her text to pictures and other artwork in which bees and bee hives were used as a frame.

There is also much lore that is associated with beekeeping, with perhaps the best-known example being the practice, in some parts of the United States and some countries in Europe, of "telling the bees" of a death in the family, especially of their master. Perhaps most important is

the popular image of bees concerning their thrift and hard work as sym-
bolized by the bee hive depicted on the state seal of Utah. The thought
that the queen of a bee hive is as important as a queen in real life is an
important consideration. However, it is the universal use of the word
"honey" as a food and as a popular term of endearment that is especially
enjoyed by those in the beekeeping trade.

---

**(2)**

# HOW TO GET STARTED IN BEEKEEPING

THERE ARE BASICALLY FIVE WAYS TO OBTAIN BEES when you want to start in beekeeping. The best method is to buy one or more secondhand colonies. A second, but definitely more expensive way is to buy package bees that are sold by the pound. Capturing unwanted swarms, a third way, can be fun and inexpensive, but it takes time. Fourth, removing bees from hollow trees or buildings can be instructive, but it too, requires time and patience and is often not successful because it is so difficult to find and protect the queen. Finally, using bait hives to collect bees is like going fishing; it can be fun but, again, is time-consuming and does not always succeed. Each of these methods is discussed in the following pages.

## THE BEST TIME OF YEAR TO START BEEKEEPING

The best time to start beekeeping is in the spring at about the time pussy willows bloom. This means January or February in the southern states and April or May in the North. By starting at this time you can follow the growth and development of your new colony through an entire season. And, with good fortune and in the right location, you may be able to harvest a honey crop in the late summer or fall.

Having said this, you may still be successful starting out at some other time of the year. There is, however, a problem with starting beekeeping in the fall in a cool climate. In such areas a colony of honey bees will need about 60 pounds of honey for the winter. While you may be able to feed bees sugar syrup to make up for any shortage, it is far easier to start a colony in the spring and let the bees gather the stores they need for winter themselves.

## BUYING HIVES OF BEES

Buying a secondhand, established colony(s) has always been the best and the cheapest way to obtain bees and start beekeeping. The advantage of buying an existing colony is that the bees should produce a honey crop in the first year you buy them. Often you can take over the location or apiary site, usually at no extra cost. Only rarely does a beekeeper own an apiary site, so an agreement must also be made with the landowner if the bees are to remain on another person's land.

Try to obtain some beekeeping advice and assistance for a few months from the seller. In fact, this may very well be the most important part of the transaction. You may, of course, move the bees to your own property, but if you don't have experience moving bees you should seek assistance from an experienced beekeeper.

It is important to buy only 10-frame Langstroth-size equipment. Ninety percent of beekeeping equipment in the United States is this size, with perhaps 5 to 8 percent of beekeepers using 8-frame Langstroth equipment. If the price is right, 8-frame equipment may be satisfactory. The 10-frame and 8-frame hive boxes (supers) hold the same size and shape frames, which are fully interchangeable. Bees in equipment of any other size should be purchased only for a pittance (if at all) and the bees transferred to modern 10-frame hives.

The physical condition of the equipment is important and affects its value. The bottomboards should not be rotted. The brood-nest supers and the frames should not be warped or pulled apart at the joints. The equipment should be well painted. The frames should not contain too much drone comb. If the equipment is not in first-class condition, is it repairable?

If the equipment is factory-made the dimensions are probably accurate; however, if it is homemade make certain the measurements are standard. It is important to check the dimensions for two reasons: the equipment must be interchangeable with any other hives that you purchase and it must have good resale value to protect your investment.

Some states require that colonies be examined for disease before they are moved or sold. Information concerning any such regulations can be obtained from your state's Department of Agriculture. There are no federal regulations concerning the inter- or intrastate movement of bees. Many states have been making changes in their regulations pertaining to bee-keeping in recent years, and there is less colony inspection on the part of state apiary inspectors than there was even a few years ago.

## BUYING PACKAGE BEES

Many beekeepers in the southern states grow worker bees that they sell by the pound (1 pound contains approximately 4,000 bees). They also grow queen honey bees that you may buy separately or with a package. A package must have both a queen and worker bees, but drones (male bees) are unnecessary. I recommend that beginners buy a 3-pound package, though 2-pound packages are sometimes satisfactory in more northern areas, especially Canada. There are more bees in a 3-pound package, and this gives greater assurance of success.

Packages should be ordered in the late fall or early spring. The bees and the queen should be put into hives at the time of the first flowering of pussy willows. This will be about April 15th to 20th across the northern tier of states and in Canada, considerably earlier in the South. Worker bees often have short life spans, sometimes only five to seven weeks long during the active season. A queen received in a package of bees will start to lay eggs a day or two after she is released from her cage. However, it takes another 21 days to grow a new worker bee from the egg. Thus, at least 22 to 23 days will elapse before any new bees are

*Two 3-pound packages of bees are pictured here. The first step after receiving the packages of bees is to paint about a pint of sugar syrup onto the screen of each one. The bees will consume this syrup within minutes.*

produced in the package bee colony; as a result, a 3-pound package that starts with 12,000 bees may contain only 7,500 to 8,000 live bees by the time the first young bees emerge. This also means that a package of bees may not grow strong enough to obtain more than the food it needs for winter; in other words, it may not produce enough honey to make harvest possible during its first year. This is one disadvantage of buying packages instead of established colonies.

*After the bees have been fed, the small, square wooden top, which holds the feeder jar in place, is removed.*

*The feeder jar and the queen cage are next removed from the package. Well-fed bees such as these are gentle.*

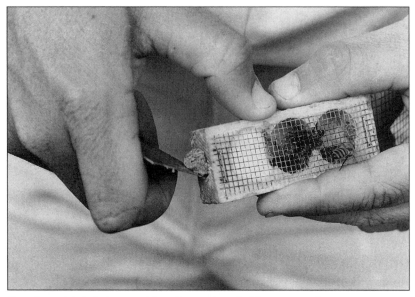

*Here the cork is being removed from the candy end of the queen cage.*

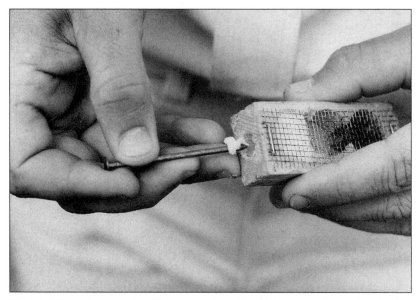

*If most of the sugar candy is still in place, some should be removed so as to speed up the time it takes the queen to be released from her cage by the bees. (Bees, from within and without, eat the candy away.)*

The queen cage is placed, candy-end up, full cage-face exposed, between two frames. The bees are then shaken from the package, after which the innercover and cover are put into place. It is difficult to dislodge all of the bees from the package. When nearly empty, the package may be placed in front of the hive and the remaining bees will crawl into the hive.

## CAPTURING SWARMS

Hiving a swarm of bees can be a thrilling experience. It is not difficult and requires only a little knowledge of beekeeping. It is not uncommon to find a swarm of bees hanging from a limb in a tree or bush in the late spring and early summer months. Once found, it is usually possible to entice the bees into accepting an artificial home.

Swarming is the natural method of colony reproduction in honey bees. Before people came onto the scene it was important for colonies of bees to swarm; otherwise, the species could not perpetuate itself. However, beekeepers do not want colonies to swarm because it takes bees away from the hive, meaning there are fewer available for honey production or pollination.

While it is easy to find a swarm in the vicinity of an apiary, don't be surprised to find a swarm almost anywhere. One of the favorite nesting locations for a swarm is in the walls of a house, especially an old house where there is space between the studs. Thus, many swarms are found in cities. Once you have found a swarm, don't delay in attempting to capture it. A swarm will move into a new home, an abandoned hive, a hollow tree, or the side of a house as soon as possible. Swarms already in a new home are difficult to remove, as is discussed below.

Bees in a swarm gorge themselves with honey before they leave the parent hive. Bees engorged with honey are gentle bees. However, if the bees have been away from their hive for some time, and because of inclement weather have been unable to gather food, they are very prone to sting. Severe stingings by honey bees are not common; those that do occur are usually the result of someone's attempting to hive a swarm that has exhausted its food supply. Swarms without food are called *dry swarms.*

You can determine if a swarm is dry by being aware of the weather conditions for the day before you try to capture it. Bees in a swarm do forage; they share their collected food with the other bees in the swarm. If the bees in a swarm have been able to forage, they will have food, and you can capture and place them in a hive without difficulty. If there has been wet and or wet and cool weather for one, two, or three days, the swarm may have exhausted its food and become dry. Even experienced beekeepers avoid dry swarms and give the bees several hours to forage in good weather before attempting to place them in a hive.

Hiving a swarm is similar to hiving a package of bees. The bees in a swarm can be placed on new foundation, thus partially eliminating the danger of disease being carried into the new hive, or the bees can be hived on old combs. Since swarms are usually hived later in the year than packages and at a time when more nectar is available, it may not be necessary to feed the bees in a swarm. However, I feel that some feeding will help. An experienced beekeeper can easily tell whether or not food is needed depending on the time of year, weather, and the nectar sources that are available at the time.

To hive a swarm it is only necessary to shake the bees from the branch on which they are found directly into a new hive. If the super used for the new hive is an old one, it will already have a bee odor, or, if there are old combs within the hive that have a bee odor, the bees will accept their new home more rapidly. Odor is very important in the social organization of the honey bee colony, and bees prefer to nest where other bees have nested before.

If the swarm of bees is on a limb close to the ground, simply bend the limb and shake the bees with one or two hard shakes into the hive after first removing the cover. If the swarm is located higher up in the tree, you have the option of either taking the new hive up a ladder to the bees or cutting off the limb on which the bees are hanging and carrying it down to the hive. If you can cut off the limb with the bees intact as a group, then you should be able to shake the bees into their new home without difficulty.

Not infrequently, bees that have been shaken into a hive will not accept their new home; they will leave the hive and the cluster may reform in the old location or a new one. Often the second time a swarm is shaken, the bees will accept the new home. As with hiving packages, you will have greater success hiving a swarm in the late afternoon or evening when the bees are less inclined to fly, and there will be less drifting between colonies.

When hiving a swarm, it is advisable to staple the bottomboard to the hive. This makes it easy to pick up the newly hived swarm at night and to move it to the apiary. It is usually not necessary to screen the entrance or to place a top screen on the hive to keep the bees inside. However, if the hive is carried inside a car, the entrance should be closed off with a screen.

## SHADE

It is a curious fact that, if given a choice, bees will select a home site that is shaded. On the other hand, beekeepers try to locate their colonies in full sunlight so as to force the bees into the field earlier in the morning and later in the afternoon. Bees with brood will not abandon their hive. We have often had bees enter a bait hive only to leave it if the sun hits it later in the day. We have no hard scientific data on this but presume that sites in full sunlight pose problems insofar as overheating is concerned. More than once we have hived a swarm in the morning or early afternoon with the intention of returning in the evening, after all of the bees are in the hive, to move it to a new location, only to find that the bees had left. Our experiments have suggested this was because of sunlight. If you hive a swarm in the morning or early afternoon, it should be pushed back under a small tree or bush so it stays out of the sunlight during the rest of the day.

## BAIT HIVES

You can easily capture swarms in boxes called *bait hives*. These should be hung on trees or poles about a week before the swarming season starts, as

*These two bait hives are well located. They are visible but shaded and at the proper height above the ground.*

bees will often scout for a homesite before the swarm leaves the parent colony.

Honey bees have definite preferences when selecting a homesite. They prefer to nest high rather than low; 15 feet above the ground appears to be optimum. Your bait hive must be visible but shaded. Once brood is present, however, bees will not abandon a hive in the sun. A small entrance, about 1¼ inches in diameter is best; the shape of the entrance is

*To remove the bees from this section of a tree that contains the nest, a cutout piece of plywood is placed over the exposed top of the nest. A super of combs, into which the bees will move slowly, and a cover, are placed above.*

not important, but bees prefer an entrance near the bottom. Bait hives catch more swarms when facing east or south. A volume of 1.4 cubic feet, about the volume of a standard 10-frame super, is best. The shape of the hive is not important. Light must not enter in from the top. We paint our bait hives green to camouflage them, but any color appears acceptable. Any type of wood is satisfactory, but bees appear to avoid new wood. Adding a small piece of old comb, even if it just lies on the bottom of the box, helps make the hive more attractive, but that may be only because its odor helps the bees to find the site. Don't leave good combs in a bait hive, because wax moths and other pests may destroy them.

## REMOVING BEES FROM A TREE OR BOX

It is possible to remove the bees found in a bee tree or box with fixed combs by one of two methods. *Fixed combs* are combs that are attached to the top and sides of the container. They are difficult to remove without damaging the comb. Considerable time and effort are required to do so, but in both cases there is much to observe and learn about bee behavior.

In the case of a bee tree, it is necessary to cut down the tree and to cut the log so as to expose the top of the nest. The portion of the tree containing the nest is then set upright again. Sometimes, felling a tree to recover that portion containing the nest so damages the comb that many bees are killed; this depends upon the size of the tree and how it is felled. When attempting to save the bees from a nest found in a box or field crate, it is again necessary to remove some of the top boards to expose the combs.

When the combs in the top of a nest in a tree or box are exposed, you can drum the bees out of their old nest, a method that can take 10 to 20 minutes. Or, you can place a super of old combs on top of the hive and let the bees move upward by themselves; this second method of transfer can take several weeks but it is easier than drumming out the bees.

Drumming is a method of moving bees from fixed comb hives that is several centuries old. If you beat rhythmically on the sides of a hive with your hands or with a hammer, the bees will soon walk upward. You can place a super or a cardboard box above the old nest and the bees will move into it. The beat need not be too fast—probably 40 to 60 beats a minute is satisfactory. Don't get too ambitious and beat too hard or too fast. The queen will usually leave the hive with the rest of the bees.

*This bee tree nest has been cut away to show the comb.*

When bees are drummed, very few of them take wing; drumming does not anger the bees. Often about 10 percent of the bees, the younger bees, may not leave the hive.

If you decide to drum a hive, you might also try to save some of the old comb. It is possible to cut the comb, especially that containing brood, from the old nest and to tie it into a frame with string. The bees will later fix the pieces of comb into place. However, such combs are seldom perfect, and you will probably end up with combs containing too many drone cells. It is probably best to save only the bees and then to render the beeswax from an old nest.

Another technique for removing bees from a fixed comb nest is to allow the bees to move upward, by themselves, into a super of combs that has been placed above the old nest. It is actually only important that the queen move upward and begin to lay eggs in the new super; if she does not do so within a week, it is usually because there is a barrier between the old nest and the new one, such as too much honey, too little comb exposed, or some other constriction. If eggs are not found in the new super within a week, you must make some effort to encourage the bees upward. This usually means exposing more of the top of the old nest.

Once the bees have moved into the new super, a queen excluder should be placed between the two units; the queen may or may not be found before this is done. If she is not found, check the hive again after four days to determine if there are eggs in the new hive. If eggs are present, the queen is present; if there are no eggs, the excluder must be removed and the operation repeated until the queen is found above her old nest.

After the queen is above the excluder, allow the brood to hatch out from the old comb below and then destroy the old nest. Allowing the bees to move upward by themselves has the added advantage of saving the emerging brood and probably results in a stronger colony of bees. As in the case of buying bees, placing bees from a fixed comb nest into a new hive is best done in the spring so that the bees have time to adjust to their new home and especially have the time necessary to gather the food they need for winter.

## RACES, VARIETIES AND STRAINS OF BEES

The honey bees we use in North America evolved in Europe, Africa, and the Near East (western Iran). On these two continents there are about 26 races of honey bees. Three of these have been favorites in North America, especially the Italian, Caucasian, and Carniolan races from Europe. The last two have been favored because they are more gentle, while the Italian bees are popular because they are more resistant to some of the diseases, most notably European foulbrood. I have had a prejudice against Caucasian bees because they tend to use so much propolis, which sticks to my fingers and makes hive manipulations difficult. Years ago, before the advent of antibiotics, when colonies were manipulated more frequently and many beekeepers still produced comb honey, there was strong pressure to use bees that collected much less propolis.

However, the accidental introduction of three new honey bee diseases (chalkbrood, tracheal mites, and varroa mites) in North America in the past few years has caused us to revise our thinking about races and their good and bad characteristics. Today we are less concerned about races; the emphasis is, first and foremost, on finding bees that are resistant to the organisms that cause disease. Once this is done we can again begin to select among the resistant bees for other desirable qualities.

---

## 3

# SPRING MANAGEMENT

HONEY BEES FOLLOW A NATURAL CYCLE OF THE year everywhere in the United States. In the northern states and Canada the active season is short, and the dates when flowers bloom, bees swarm, and so forth are predictable within a few days. In the southern states, however, the active bee season may be stretched over almost the entire year, and hence these dates are much less precise.

The population in a colony increases in the spring and decreases in the fall. At some point, usually during a three-week period in the late spring, summer, or fall, bees in a colony gather 50 percent or more of the honey they will use as food for the whole year; the rest of the honey they need is gathered over an only slightly longer period. To make money in beekeeping one must understand this annual cycle and seek to maximize honey production during the time that nectar is available. Those who rent bees for pollination must seek to use this honey flow, and the energy it provides, to grow bees that may be rented. In this chapter we discuss the natural cycle of the year.

In almost all parts of the United States, colonies of honey bees have the least amount of brood in October and November. An exception to this rule is southernmost Florida, where a fall honey flow from the Brazilian pepper and melaleuca (sometimes called cajeput or punk tree) stimulates brood rearing; and curiously, there may even be swarming at this time of year in the area. Brazilian pepper has become an increasingly important honey plant in a ring of islands starting with Bermuda, ranging into the Caribbean and on to Hawaii.

Egg laying on the part of the queen starts in the whole country in late December. I believe the stimulus for this, and the reason there is generally less brood rearing in the fall, is because an increasing day length (or *photoperiod*) stimulates brood rearing while a decreasing day length slows or brings it to a halt. While I have found no data to conclusively prove this thought, the cycle of the honey bee's year fits closely with changing day-length patterns. For example, there is almost no swarming in the summer soon after the longest day of the year on June 21. Honey bees can rear some brood using body reserves and stored pollen and honey. However, fresh pollen is the real stimulus for maximizing brood rearing. Thus, sometime in January we see heavy brood rearing across the southern tips of the country, but it is not until early April that brood rearing gets into full swing across the northern states and Canada.

## THE FIRST SPRING INSPECTION

The purpose of the first early spring inspection is to check for food, to pick up dead colonies, and to combine weak colonies. While colony entrances can be checked occasionally throughout the winter, it is not until January in the southern states, and April in the northern states, that it is possible to make sure that colonies have wintered satisfactorily and have sufficient food. Most beekeepers prefer to delay opening their colonies until about two weeks after the first spring pollen is available. In fact, it is a reasonably correct assumption that, if bees from a colony are gathering pollen, the colony is in good condition, except for the possible danger of being short of honey.

The first inspection of a colony should be brief, especially if the temperature is cool. The best guide is to inspect colonies only at a time when it is warm enough for the bees to fly, usually 65° to 70°F. The colonies should be unpacked if they had been given some winter protection. Check bottomboards and innercovers to make sure they are dry; if not, they should be replaced. Heft the colony to determine if it has sufficient food; in the spring a colony should have a minimum of 20 pounds of honey and hopefully more. It is probably not wise to inspect the brood nest this early in the season unless you have some special reason for doing so: chilling of the brood can occur and cause much loss to the colony if your inspection is too lengthy; in the North wait until May to check the equipment and colony condition more carefully.

In the fall we usually reduce a colony's entrance with a block or strip of wood that is called an entrance cleat. The entrance cleat should remain in place for at least a month after the colony is unpacked in the spring. The cleat is removed, or the entrance made larger, when there appears to be any signs of congestion at the entrance. The size of the entrance needed will depend upon the population of the colony. Knowing when to remove a cleat, or make the entrance larger, is part of the artistry of beekeeping.

Dead colonies should be carefully inspected to determine why they died; depending upon the area, American foulbrood, mites, or some other disease may be the cause of the colonies' dying in the winter. Weak colonies should be combined, either with strong colonies or other weak colonies; they can then be split at a later date and given new queens. Trying to carry a weak colony through the spring buildup period is not worth the effort and is often futile. Combine colonies by setting one on top of another with only a sheet of newspaper between the two brood nests; then cut three or four slits in the paper with your hive tool. The queens will eventually fight, and, usually, the stronger of the two survives.

*It is best to unite weak colonies in the spring. This is done by placing a single piece of newspaper, with a few slits, between the two units. The newspaper slows the time it takes the bees in the two hives to meet, and this eliminates fighting between them.*

## SPRING FEEDING

A colony that produces 100 pounds of surplus honey collects nearly twice that amount for its own use during the year. A general recommendation is that a colony of honey bees should have 15 to 20 pounds of honey in reserve at all times of the year, and, of course, much more than that in winter.

In many parts of the United States colonies can suffer from a lack of food in the late spring. This is especially true in the North, where there may be a dearth of nectar near the middle or end of May following the dandelion and yellow rocket bloom. It may be two or three weeks before the clovers begin to flower and yield nectar. While there may be some plants in flower during this period, they are relatively few and far between. When a colony of honey bees goes into a starvation condition, their first reaction is to remove the larvae and discard them in front of the hive. The queen continues to lay eggs, but as they hatch, these larvae, too, are discarded. Eventually, of course, the adult bees starve, though they can subsist for a certain amount of time on body reserves. The overall effect of this spring starvation is to weaken the colony. Because bees rear large quantities of brood during May and June, they also consume large quantities of honey, and it is important that you be alert as to the food reserves in the colonies.

Many beekeepers save combs of honey from the fall for spring feeding. This is probably the easiest way to feed bees, since only one inspection of the colony is necessary, at which time one or more combs can be inserted. An added advantage of feeding honey this way is that old capped honey has little odor and will usually not stimulate robbing. If you spill sugar syrup on the ground in the apiary during the process of feeding, it is possible that robbing may be stimulated, especially if there are very few flowers in bloom. When honey is not available for spring feeding, you should definitely use sugar syrup. In the fall, when bees are prepared for winter and sugar syrup is fed, the syrup mixture is made up of two parts sugar and one part water by weight or measure; for spring feeding the ratio should be one part sugar to one part water.

There are several ways to feed sugar syrup to bees. The two methods most widely used are the division board feeder and feeder pails or jars that are put over the top of the colony. Both appear to work equally well. Beekeepers who routinely feed in the spring sometimes leave their division board feeders in the colony all year round.

*This colony is being fed using 1-gallon glass jars, which are filled with syrup and inverted over the top bars of the frames.*

Another method of feeding sugar syrup is to pour it directly into the combs and to insert combs filled with sugar syrup along the edge of the brood nest or above or below the brood nest. Sugar syrup can be poured into the combs in the home apiary or honey house and then carried to the field with minimal loss. If you try this method use a sprinkler can or a pail with many holes in it; a solid stream of syrup poured onto a comb will not penetrate the cells. Pour the sugar syrup into both sides of the comb, then give the comb a good shake over a water tub or similar receptacle to catch the surplus syrup. If you do this, only a very small quantity of the sugar syrup will drip out of the comb while you are transporting it to the apiary.

Some beekeepers recommend feeding dry sugar. Bees will eat dry sugar if there is a dearth of nectar and they are on the verge of starvation. A few pounds of dry sugar can prevent starvation, and dry sugar should be used if absolutely nothing else is available. However, it is also a fact that bees will often carry dry sugar out of the hive and discard it in front. When other sources of nectar become available, bees will usually cease to collect or store the dry sugar that has been placed on the innercover or bottomboard of the colony. Bees must also collect water to liquefy the sugar in order to use it for food, and this places a small strain on the colony.

Small entrance feeders for colonies, such as Boardman feeders, are not recommended except in emergencies, and even then they are usually useless. Colonies that need feeding usually require far more food than can be fed through a Boardman or entrance feeder. Furthermore, entrance feeders get cold at night; the bees will cease feeding from them shortly before sunset and will not feed again until there is warm weather. During inclement weather they will not feed from them at all. Entrance feeders give beekeepers an opportunity to observe how much food their bees are taking; they are used by a few beekeepers in the warm, southern states but are generally of little value.

### Feeding pollen substitutes and supplements

Pollen provides bees with the protein they need. In the beekeeping literature you will find references to both pollen substitutes and pollen supplements. Don't confuse these two terms. A *pollen substitute* is a material used in place of pollen. A *pollen supplement* is usually the same material, but with previously bee-collected pollen added in varying amounts.

Feeding pollen supplements and substitutes is recommended more in some areas of the country than others. In many states one of the major limiting factors to beekeeping is the shortage of pollen at certain times of the year. For instance, beekeepers in some parts of the Southwest have found that pollen supplements are especially helpful. In other areas of the country bees may collect so much pollen as to become *pollen bound* (to have too much pollen), and on rare occasions beekeepers have been known to actually discard combs of pollen. In the northern United States bees usually collect pollen in sufficient quantity throughout the active season, so that it is not necessary to feed pollen substitutes or supplements. In certain of the midwestern states these materials are recommended, but this is largely because some beekeepers in those areas use two-queen colonies and try to build larger populations of bees, especially in the early spring.

Generally speaking, feeding pollen supplements and substitutes is not advised for beekeepers in the northern United States, but opinions on this matter vary widely. The major reason for not feeding pollen supplements and substitutes is that it is not usually necessary.

Research on pollen supplements and substitutes indicates that soybean flour is satisfactory as bee food. The material is not too attractive to bees, however, and for this reason adding bee-collected pollen to it is advisable. There are various methods of storing bee-collected pollen, including freezing it, drying it, and mixing it with sugar; probably the easiest and best way to store bee-collected pollen is in a home freezer.

Adding honey to a pollen supplement will make it more attractive to bees; however, there is a real danger in using honey instead of sugar syrup, since it is possible to transmit disease in this way. If you are certain that there is no disease in an apiary, then adding honey might prove helpful.

## CLEAN EQUIPMENT AND GOOD COMBS

Replacing worn and warped equipment, broken combs, and combs with too much drone comb, as well as scraping and cleaning hive bodies, innercovers, and other equipment are jobs most easily done in the spring. At that time of the year there are fewer bees in the hive and changes can be made with the least difficulty. Keeping equipment in good condition facilitates work in the apiary during the active season.

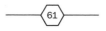

*This picture shows a very good brood pattern in a comb with all worker cells.*

*A mediocre brood pattern is illustrated in this picture. Too many cells are empty.*

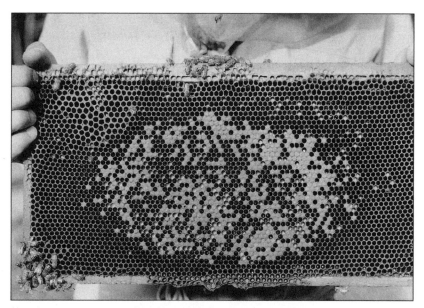

*Here is a very poor, spotty brood pattern indicating a poor queen or a disease.*

During the course of the year bees collect and bring a large amount of propolis into the hive. Propolis, also known as "bee glue," is a red-brown resinous substance that bees collect from plants or tree buds and use to strengthen combs and patch up cracks. An accumulation of propolis, together with an excess of burr comb, can slow manipulations and the removal of combs from a hive. Protruding pieces of burr comb can also kill or maim some bees as frames are removed from a super for inspection.

While it is normal for a colony of bees to contain some drones, the drone population should be kept to a minimum, as drones serve no useful function other than to mate with virgin queens. The easiest way to control the drone population is to have good frames with a maximum number of worker cells in the brood nest. The best frames are made when full sheets of foundation are used. (See "Adding foundation and making new combs" in Chapter 4.)

While replacing worn equipment and keeping good combs may appear to be minor aspects of spring management, it is part of the routine of careful management that leads to the production of a maximum crop.

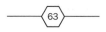

*The bees in this colony are congested and are "hanging out." This colony must be given more room or it will swarm.*

## SWARMING AND THE CYCLE OF THE YEAR

After the control of diseases, preventing swarming is the most difficult task you will face as a beekeeper. This is especially true in the northern states and Canada, as swarming becomes more intense as one moves north. In Florida and the other southern states, swarming can occur during any of the spring months, but it is not the problem it is farther north. In part this is because colonies in the North usually contain more bees and are more crowded at the peak of the season.

Swarm control is an important, and often the most frustrating, part of spring management. In the early spring your chief concern is that colonies have survived the winter and have started to increase their populations in preparation for the first honey flow. Young queens, food, equipment, disease control, and locations are all important in this regard.

However, once the colony is over this early building period, you are faced with the other extreme—colonies that are too populous and are about to swarm. Swarming is a natural process. Without swarming, or colony division, the species cannot survive. Reproduction of individuals within the colony itself is not sufficient; there must also be a reproduction of colonies. Only populous colonies will swarm under normal circumstances. Therefore, if you build colonies with large numbers of bees, which is necessary to secure the largest crop, you are also creating conditions conducive to swarming. This is a simple fact that you must accept and around which your management program should be built.

From the practical point of view, swarming should be prevented. However, what you will have to do depends upon the condition of your colonies and whether or not signs of swarm preparation are evident. Not all colonies of bees will swarm, even though, outwardly, conditions appear to be similar. In such cases the beekeeper's skill in diagnosing what is taking place inside the hive is important.

Determining whether or not a colony will swarm is done by observing the construction of queen cups and queen cells in or adjacent to the brood rearing area. Where colonies are kept in two or more standard Langstroth supers, following the development of cups and cells is most easily accomplished by tilting the upper super upward and forward and looking at the bottom bars of the exposed frames. Since there is a space between the supers, and this space is still in the brood nest, this is the most likely place where cups and cells will be built.

### Swarm control versus swarm prevention

*Swarm prevention* is concerned with those steps taken to deter or prevent queen-cell construction within a colony; *swarm control* involves the steps you take after queen cells containing larvae are found. There is a profound difference between these two conditions. It is not too difficult to prevent a colony from building queen cells; however, once a colony has queen cells with larvae, it is difficult to stop the colony from building more cells and swarming. Therefore, you should do everything possible to prevent queen-cell construction: colonies that swarm are useless for honey production in the year they swarm because of their depleted field force.

A queen cell is difficult to define. In its early stages it is called a *queen cup*. A queen cup is the name for the cell before it has an egg in it or when it contains only an egg. When the egg in the cup hatches, it is then called a *queen cell*; this is also because changes in the cell itself become evident at the same time. About the time the egg hatches, the bees begin to add wax to the edges of the cup and lengthen it. Swarm-prevention methods are usually successful when applied to colonies with queen cups containing eggs but are rarely successful when applied to colonies with two-day-old larvae in queen cups. Once the larvae are two or more days old, only swarm-control measures are satisfactory. (When the larvae is only one day old the process can go either way.)

The mere presence of queen cells does not always mean that a colony will swarm. Swarming and/or queen rearing by a colony can be abortive. However, a colony with queen cells will usually swarm or *supersede* (i.e., replace the old queen). What starts out as swarming may become supersedure, and vice versa. It is generally accepted that colonies with one to six queen cells are more likely to supersede their queen than to swarm. Colonies with four to twenty cells are more likely to swarm. These overlapping figures are intentional. The size, shape, and position of the cells in a colony also give clues as to what might happen. Generally, when the queen cells are larger, with rougher surfaces, and more on the periphery of the brood nest, swarming is indicated. Smaller cells, built closer to the center of the brood nest, indicate supersedure. However, these are only general rules of thumb. In addition to normal colony variations, certain races of bees tend to build more queen cells than others under apparently the same circumstances.

The swarming season varies as one goes from south to north. Close to the equator, colonies can swarm from February through June, depending upon the food available to the colony. In New York State swarming can occur in May or June, rarely later. While colonies have been known to swarm in August and September, such swarms are not too common. Our data show that about 20 percent of colonies may swarm in the fall in New York State, but this may not be true everywhere, even in the North. Usually the presence of queen cells after the normal swarming season indicates that the colony is about to supersede its queen.

Clipping a queen's wings is neither a swarm-control nor a swarm-prevention technique. It is not recommended except when you are interested in comb honey production. Clipping a queen's wings may delay swarming, but it will not stop it. Usually a colony that swarms leaves the hive within a few days after the queen cells are capped. The bees will attempt to

*The underside of a super is a good place to check for open queen cups, of which there are 12 here clearly hanging downward. (A few others are less distinct.)*

leave even though the queen cannot fly; however, as soon as the bees find that the queen cannot depart with them, they return to the original hive. Often a colony will attempt to swarm several times under these conditions; finally, the swarm will depart with the first virgin queen to emerge.

### Methods of swarm prevention

To make honey you must build up your colonies to a maximum population prior to the honey flow. To do so, and to prevent swarming, requires skill and knowledge in both the art and the science of beekeeping. Proportionally, large populations of bees gather more honey than do small populations; for example, a colony with a population of 60,000 bees will gather more than twice as much honey as two colonies with 30,000 bees each. (At the same time, there is no proof that a colony with a population of 150,000 to 200,000 bees will produce more than twice as much honey as colonies half that size. In this regard, a colony with 50,000 to 60,000 bees appears to be optimum. This may be true because a queen, at least apparently, is capable of producing secretions in amounts sufficient for approximately this number of bees.) Larger populations are presumably more efficient in controlling hive temperature, humidity, guarding, and other hive tasks than are smaller populations of honey bees. For this reason alone, you should take all the steps possible to prevent swarming, for swarming divides a strong colony into two or more units.

While we still have much to learn about the causes and biology of swarming, there is agreement among researchers and practical beekeepers on the primary cause of swarming. The consensus is that swarming is caused by congestion, especially a congestion of bees in the brood nest. The practical swarming-prevention measures used today are aimed at alleviating congestion within this area of the hive.

The best way to prevent swarming is to take steps that will relieve congestion, especially congestion within the brood nest. There are three basic techniques: reversing; adding supers (sometimes accompanied with reversing and/or raising a frame of brood above the existing brood nest); and the Demaree method of swarm prevention (also sometimes used for swarm control).

Reversing, when one has a colony in two supers, is the simplest of the swarm-prevention methods. The first reversing (some beekeepers may

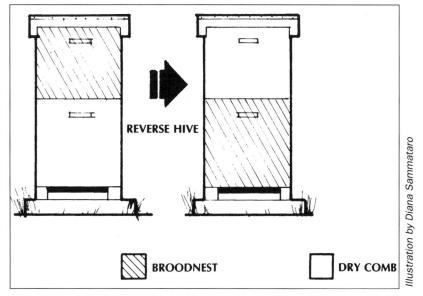

REVERSE HIVE

BROODNEST

DRY COMB

Illustration by Diana Sammataro

*Reversing Supers*

reverse three to five times at about two-week intervals before the primary honey flow) usually takes place in early May in New York State. A queen honey bee has a tendency to work upward in the colony as she is laying eggs. Thus, the upper super usually becomes crowded with brood (and sometimes food, too) while the lower super remains relatively empty. By reversing the two supers that comprise the brood nest, the beekeeper makes space available for more egg laying above the existing (or filled) super. Consequently, the queen has additional room to move in an upward direction. Reversing also, temporarily at least, splits the existing brood nest. These two measures, making room available above and splitting the existing brood nest, relieve the immediate congestion and deter the construction of queen cups and, later, queen cells.

The second method of swarm prevention—adding supers—has at least two variations. Often just adding a super above the two existing supers in early spring (as early as February in the Deep South and as late as early May in the North) is sufficient to relieve congestion. Depending upon the position of the brood nest in the super below, this gives the bees the room they need and provides the queen with space for increased egg laying. However, just adding supers may not be enough. Since bees store food above their brood nest, not below it, there is often a barrier of pollen and honey above an existing nest when the third super is added. Therefore, it is usually advisable to reverse the bottom supers at the same time, and to raise one frame of brood into the center of the third super and to place the empty comb it replaces into the center of the brood nest below. While this spreads the brood nest—an act to be avoided if the weather is cool and there is danger of chilling the brood—it is an excellent method of relieving congestion.

The third method of swarm prevention is the so-called Demaree method; it is also a popular swarm-control measure. It has been written about in several journals and texts. Basically the method involves confining the queen in the lowest super with a *queen excluder* and placing the brood frames in the third or fourth super above the bottomboard. This drastic separation of queen and brood is perhaps the best of the swarm-prevention methods were it not for the time involved in finding the queen and making the switch of the brood to the upper chamber. Even the best beekeeper cannot make such a manipulation in less than 10 minutes, and it is not a practical method on a commercial basis; however, for the hobbyist it may well be a practical and sound method of colony management. The only danger is that, as a result of this separation, the bees may build queen cells in the brood placed in the top super; you must inspect the elevated brood to remove any existing queen cells five to seven days after the original manipulation.

### Methods of swarm control

Once queen cells with larvae are found within a colony in the swarming season, you must take strong measures to prevent the colony from swarming. Cutting out queen cells is considered by some an effective swarm-control measure, but in fact this is not so. Queen cells are visually striking and easy to identify; however, their very presence is evidence, and final evidence, of a more complicated biological process that is going on within the colony. Cutting out queen cells can slow swarming, but as soon as the cells are cut out and removed, the bees will usually just build more.

Infrequently, a colony will even swarm after the queen cells have been removed; this occurs when the cells are cut within a day or a few

hours of the time swarming would have taken place normally. The greatest danger in cutting out queen cells is that you can miss one, with the result that swarming takes place anyway. Comb honey producers crowd their colonies to force the bees to work in the small, crowded confines of a comb honey section. This encourages swarming. Comb honey producers cut queen cells, when they are present, every seven or eight days. They also clip the wings of the queens in their colonies so that, if a swarm emerges, it will return to the parent hive. If a comb honey producer misses a queen cell under these conditions, the swarm will leave with the virgin queen when she emerges. Even comb honey producers find it is not profitable to remove queen cells more than about three times; after the third time (and colonies are carefully marked in this regard), a colony that persists in constructing queen cells is requeened or used for other purposes.

The presence of queen cells is only one manifestation of the swarming process. Research has shown that many other things occur in the colony at the same time. For example, queen bees lose about one-third of their weight during the four to five days prior to the time the swarm emerges from the hive; this weight loss is necessary so that the queen can fly, for otherwise she is too heavy to do so. Such a weight loss obviously affects egg laying and other queen activities. There is also increasing evidence to show that foraging slows during the several days prior to swarming; large numbers of bees engorge in preparation for swarming and this, too, occurs several days prior to the time the swarm actually emerges. Thus, swarming does more than divide a colony; it robs the colony of bees at a time when having a strong, populous colony is necessary to gather honey.

When queen cells are found in a colony, there are only three basic methods of swarm control, each with some variations, which may be used to prevent swarming: removal of the queen, removal of the brood, and separation of the queen and brood. You can also split the colony into two parts, requeening the queenless half or allowing it to rear its own queen. However, this is nothing more than artificial swarming and creates two weaker units that will not be able to produce as much honey had the colony not been divided.

Separation of the brood and queen involves the Demaree method, described above, and can be used in either swarm prevention or swarm control. One popular variation of this swarm-control technique is to give

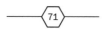

the brood above the old colony a new queen, thereby creating a two-queen colony. The two units are later combined, just before the honey flow, so as to produce a populous colony for honey production. The old queen can be killed before the two units are united, or the two can be put together, allowing the two queens to fight; in this case the younger queen usually survives. There are also several variations of this so-called two-queen system of management. Generally speaking, this method is too time-consuming for use in the northern United States; also, there is often a serious food shortage between late May and mid-June, after the dandelion and yellow rocket honey flows and before the major honey flow begins in June.

Removal of the brood, or of the queen, is likewise a drastic step, one which, if not done properly, can weaken the colony so much that a surplus of honey will not be gathered. Dr. C. C. Miller, whose books on comb honey production contain the best bee management information available, recommends caging a queen for a week or ten days to control swarming. This has the same effect as removing the queen. This interruption stops egg laying and relieves congestion. At the same time, it usually prevents the construction of additional queen cells, though it is still necessary to cut out those that have already been built.

Depending upon the strength of the colony, it may be necessary to remove only a few frames of brood and to replace them with empty combs in the center of the brood nest. This step, too, must be accompanied with cutting out the queen cells that already have been built. It involves a separation of the brood nest—a dangerous practice if cool weather prevails, for brood can be chilled and killed. The person who successfully practices the art of beekeeping takes the necessary steps at precisely the right time. Experience is the best guide. No two colonies and no two seasons are alike; this provides a constant challenge to the beekeepers in their efforts to maintain strong colonies for honey production.

## SUPERING

Giving colonies extra supers of combs before the honey flow aids in swarm control, though supering offers other advantages to the beekeeper, too. While most beekeepers can judge when a honey flow will take place, it is not always possible to do so. For this reason alone you should always make cer-

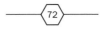

tain the colonies have adequate room for nectar storage. In addition, supers of combs that are placed on strong colonies will not be attacked by wax moths or other pests, provided the colonies are sufficiently strong.

When you want to produce liquid (extracted) honey, you should add new supers on top of the hive. This means adding empty supers on top of already filled supers and is called *top-supering*. When comb honey is being produced, the new comb honey supers are placed underneath the already filled, or partially filled supers, and immediately on top of the brood nest. This is called *bottom-supering* and is a basic difference in colony management between the two types of honey production. Some people argue that bottom-supering is helpful in liquid honey production because it places empty comb close to the brood nest, in a position where it is readily accessible. This is probably true, but most beekeepers do not consider it too important and the lifting involved is hard work.

## ROUTINE SITE MAINTENANCE

If you have only one apiary, and it is adjacent to your residence, the site is usually mowed and tended with the rest of the home grounds. There is one note of caution about mowing around bee hives with mowers that have gasoline engines. For some reason the noise, the odor, or the ground vibrations emanating from a gasoline engine irritates the bees, and they are prone to fly out and sting anyone pushing the mower in front of the hive. It is a good idea not to work the colonies while or immediately after there is mowing at the apiary site. It is also advisable to mow the grass around colonies early in the morning or late in the evening, when the bees are not so active and not so easily disturbed.

Reducing the amount of grass around a colony can be done by placing a piece of protruding tarpaper or roofing paper underneath the hive stand. If the tarpaper protrudes two to four inches, you can mow around the hive stand with ease and there will be no accumulation of grass there. Likewise, the tarpaper will prevent the grass from growing up between the colonies on a hive stand.

Beekeepers with remote apiaries find that they usually mow them less frequently. However, the grass in front of the colonies should be prevented from growing so as to not block their entrances. This can be done by using black paper left over from wrapping the hives in the winter, which can be tucked under the hive stand and can extend out from the colony two or three feet and be held in place with stones. If the growth of grass around your colonies is not somehow controlled, the colonies will become shaded and flight to and from the colonies will be impeded.

# 4

# SUMMER MANAGEMENT

I T IS DURING THE SUMMER THAT BEEKEEPERS REAP THE rewards of good fall, winter, and spring management. Summer management of honey bees is often more a matter of hard work than the application of good judgment; in the summer, the colonies are heavy with honey (or at least they should be), and many of the practices are routine and involved with harvesting the crop. Still, there are certain items that should receive attention as apiaries are visited and colonies inspected. These are discussed in this chapter.

## THE PRIMARY HONEY FLOW

In most areas in the northern United States the honey flow from clovers

*Using a hive on scales is an excellent way of following the progress of a honey flow. It is especially exciting when a colony gains 5 to 10 pounds a day, something that occurs only on a small number of days each year.*

and alfalfa, starting sometimes in mid or late June and lasting usually through July, is the flow from which the most and the best-quality honey is made. Thus, it is called the *primary honey flow*. For a profitable commercial beekeeping operation, the primary flow should produce a surplus of 100 pounds per hive. In recent years, in certain parts of the Northeast, the honey flow from alfalfa has been the most important component of the primary honey flow. Each honey-producing area in the country has at least one primary honey flow, though in some areas there may be a second honey flow as good as the primary one. The term "primary honey flow" is especially helpful when one thinks about management schemes.

Keeping records of honey flows over a period of years will help you to establish which honey flow is most important in your local area. At the same time you must be aware of changing conditions in your area. In some parts of the North, goldenrod, which starts to yield nectar in August, is of prime consequence. This is especially true where clover is no longer grown in quantity for dairying. In such areas it is often advisable to split your colonies early in the year into two or three units, and then to build them up to maximum strength by about the first of August. Thus, there is no exact management scheme for the primary honey flow. It varies from area to area and, to some extent, from year to year. Accurate record keeping is the best way to estimate when and what should be done in future years; a hive on scales is probably a good investment for most beekeepers.

## QUEEN EXCLUDERS

Some beekeepers feel that a *queen excluder* is indispensable to their management systems; others feel it is a nuisance and/or a "honey excluder", which may interfere with normal ventilation in the colony. In my opinion a queen excluder has more advantages than disadvantages, if properly used. Excluders work well in hives where *bee escapes* (see Chapter 5) are used, too, as well as in other management systems.

Queen excluders should not be put on colonies any earlier in the season than necessary; they seldom serve any useful purpose before July 8th in the North. Remove the excluders as soon as possible in the fall; this is usually done at the same time the fall honey is removed. While some beekeepers put the queen excluder above the second super, it is best to put the queen into the bottom chamber and to place the excluder above this single chamber. There are several reasons for doing so. Usually by July 8th in the northern states the bottomboard chamber is empty. Thus, if the queen is forced to lay in the super, she normally has plenty of room. (A standard frame contains 6,000 to 7,000 cells; since a queen can lay a maximum of about 1,500 eggs a day, she can be forced to do all of her egg laying in one standard super.) Secondly, if the queen is prevented from laying in the second brood chamber, the bees will fill it with honey, and, when the colony is wintered, it will have a full super of good-quality honey for winter food. Usually, the quality of the honey gathered in July in the North is superior to that gathered in August or September; it is therefore better for winter food.

The chief question about excluders is what is the easiest and most efficient way to put the queens down; certainly it is too time-consuming a process to search for and find the queen and then to place her below the excluder. This method may be practical for someone who has only a few colonies, but not for the beekeeper who has more.

There are basically three methods of forcing a queen into the lower chamber: driving the bees down with a repellent; smoking the colony heavily and forcing the bulk of the bees and the queen down; and shaking the bees and the queen off the brood combs, either in front of the colony or into the bottom super. Sometimes a combination of these methods is used. None of these methods is perfect, though using a repellent is probably the safest and easiest. A danger of shaking is that the queen may be damaged.

## HOW MANY SUPERS TO ADD?

At the end of the honey-producing season, when the crop is ready to be removed, the best colonies will be in four to seven supers. This does not mean that they will have two to five supers full of honey above the double brood nest; it merely means that they will have some bees and some honey in this number of supers. When you produce liquid honey, you expect that not every comb will be completely filled. This is quite different from comb-honey production; when making comb honey the colonies must be extremely crowded.

When you produce liquid honey, it is best to have more than enough supers on the colonies. There is no absolute rule to follow, and this fact is one of the great fascinations in beekeeping. Generally beekeepers will have one or two more supers on their colonies than the bees actually need in the average year. This means, too, that occasionally you can expect to fill all the supers and to produce a bumper crop.

## ADDING FOUNDATION AND MAKING NEW COMBS

It is good beekeeping practice to make a few new combs each year. Not only do cells in the comb become smaller with each cycle of brood because of the accumulated pupal skins (cocoons), but also combs become worn and broken with age; old combs often contain too many drone cells, and combs that have not been wired properly can sag and stretch the cells.

The best time for bees to draw foundation or to make new combs is during a honey flow. While it is true that bees can draw foundation at

*Honey bees have four pairs of wax glands located on the underside of their abdomens. These wax scales have been teased out slightly from the wax mirrors onto which the wax is first secreted.*

almost any time during the active season, especially if they are fed sugar syrup, they do the best job during a flow. The best place in the hive to put new frames with foundation is just above the brood nest. Probably the ideal situation is to place six new frames with foundation in the center of the second super with an excluder on top and the queen below. The four outside combs, those in addition to the six new frames, would be drawn comb.

The second best way to draw foundation is to place four new combs, spaced alternately between five drawn combs, or to place an entire super of foundation frames immediately above the super in which the bees are storing nectar at the time the new combs are being put on the hive. Some beekeepers make a practice of including one or two new combs in every, or almost every, super as they are added to the hive during the honey flow.

The reason that new foundation should be added during the honey flow is that bees have a tendency to chew the edges of the wax foundation if nectar is not readily available. This is one of the reasons, too, that sections for comb honey production are not added until the honey flow is under way. Of course, foundation, or partially drawn comb, is never left in a hive through winter.

Great care should be taken in extracting new combs. It is best to remove much of the new cells when uncapping new combs. Often the uncapping knife is forced to cut so deep that only ¼ to ½ inch of cell wall, in depth, is left. In this way much of the weight is removed and there is less danger of breaking the comb in the extracting process. When new combs are extracted, the machine should be run very slowly so as not to put unnecessary pressure on the comb.

### *Plastic foundation*

Since 1978, when the first practical plastic foundation with high cell walls was introduced, it has found increasing favor among beekeepers, especially those with high labor costs and migratory beekeepers who must keep to tight schedules. Coating the plastic foundation with beeswax is not necessary. The high cell walls help to guide the bees in comb building.

The cheapest way to make a new comb is to place four horizontal wires in the frame and to use a sheet of heavy brood foundation. However,

when labor costs are high, or if the beekeeper has little time, my experience is that the all-plastic foundation with high cell walls works very well.
The best time to put new plastic foundation on a colony is during a honey
flow; the bees will do a better job of comb-building then, just as they do
with wax foundation.

## 5

# REMOVING THE HONEY CROP

A S SOON AS THE HONEY FLOW IS FINISHED, AND THE combs are filled with new honey, they should be removed and the honey extracted. An important reason that extracting should not be delayed is that some honeys crystallize rapidly and, once they do so, it is extremely difficult to remove them from the comb. Some of the honeys produced by fall flowers, especially aster, are notorious for their rapid crystallization rates. It is not unusual for aster honey to crystallize within ten to twenty days after being stored in a comb.

It is especially important to remove comb honey sections as soon as they are finished, as they may become travel-stained by bits of pollen and propolis from the feet of bees that walk over the comb surface. Comb honey sections lose much of their attractiveness if they are not removed as soon as possible after they have been finished by the bees.

## WHEN IS HONEY RIPE?

Honey bees collect nectar from flowers and convert it into honey by adding two chemicals (enzymes) and removing water. The chief sugar in nectar is sucrose (the same sugar that is in cane sugar). The bees convert this sucrose into glucose and fructose, but we needn't be too concerned with this process, as it goes along smoothly without any assistance from the beekeeper.

However, removing the excess moisture from honey is sometimes another matter. Honey bees usually, but not always, ripen honey to our satisfaction. Nectar may contain 50 to 85 percent water. Properly ripened honey contains less than 18.6 percent honey moisture. If the honey has a higher moisture content, it may ferment. There are laboratory instruments

*Honey bees ripen honey (remove water) by forcing warm, dry air into the hive at one point and out at another, as is illustrated by the fluttering piece of tissue paper held by the forceps at this colony entrance.*

for determining the moisture content of honey, and these are used by honey buyers and at honey shows. However, from a practical point of view, the best guide is the capping of the honey cells by the bees. Honey bees rarely build wax cappings over honey that is not fully ripe and/or has a high moisture content. Generally speaking, a comb of honey that is two-thirds or more capped is properly ripened.

Of course, ripe honey may pick up moisture, or high humidity may make it difficult for the bees to remove the moisture from the honey. There is no perfect way to determine when honey is ripe without instruments, but in most cases you can be guided by a knowledge of the weather and the extent to which the bees have capped the combs.

## METHODS OF REMOVING HONEY FROM COLONIES

There are several ways of removing supers of honey from a colony of bees. These include brushing or shaking the bees from the combs, placing bee escapes under the full supers, driving the bees with repellents, and the use of forced air. Each of these methods has its advantages and disadvan-

*This commercial beekeeper uses a motorized bag truck to move supers full of honey into a closed van. Using a closed van helps reduce robbing.*

tages, and there is no general agreement in the beekeeping industry as to which is best. Even commerical beekeepers use different methods.

Since honey is usually removed after the honey flow, and at a time when only a limited amount of nectar may be available, robbing may be stimulated. During a dearth of nectar, just the odor of exposed honey is apparently enough to trigger robbing. At the time the combs and/or supers are being removed from the hives you should take great care to keep all the new honey covered or screened so that robbing will not be encouraged.

### The bee escape

The Porter bee escape was invented in 1891. The metal bee escapes now on the market fit into the hole in a standard innercover. Innercovers with bee escapes in place are technically called "bee escape boards," though bee-keepers refer to them as "bee escapes," or sometimes just "escapes." Although the bee escape is an excellent way to remove honey from colonies of bees, there are two disadvantages. The first is that two trips must be made to the apiary, one to put the bee escapes in place and the second to remove the honey; secondly, if there are holes in the supers

*Here we see two beekeepers lifting off the full supers of honey while a third beekeeper removes the queen excluder, which he will replace with a bee escape.*

above the bee escape, bees from other hives may rob the honey from the supers. However, despite these two problems, the use of bee escapes remains a popular method of removing honey supers and is used by both hobbyists and commercial beekeepers.

A knowledge of bee behavior is helpful when bee escapes are used. If there is dripping honey above the bee escape, the bees will be more reluctant to leave the supers. Therefore, if you are removing more than one super of honey above an escape, it is helpful if the individual supers are not broken apart. Usually two people are required to lift the supers of honey with hive lifters, while a third person inserts the bee escape. However, experienced beekeepers have also found they can break the hive apart at the point where they wish to insert the bee escape by using a hive tool, then partially put the escape in position and, holding the supers with their hands, push the escape into place with their stomachs.

Experienced beekeepers with equipment that contains holes and/or cracks through which bees can rob honey have found that, if they put the escapes on early in the day, or no later than midmorning, they can remove the supers the following morning before any robbing can start. However, this is possible only if there is no dripping honey or broken combs above the escape that might delay the departure of the bees. If one delays in removing supers to which other bees can gain access, the robber bees can remove all of the honey within a few hours.

It is important to remember that bees will not abandon brood. If there is brood above a bee escape, some worker bees will remain with it; for this reason many beekeepers who use bee escapes also use queen excluders so that there is no brood in the honey storage supers.

Bee escapes can be left in place for two days or more, usually without any difficulty except for robbing. There is a slight danger of the combs above a bee escape overheating and melting during very warm weather because there is no ventilation. All the advantages and disadvantages must be weighed by the prospective user. One great advantage of using a bee escape is that you may start to remove your honey very early in the morning, before the bees fly, and do so without wearing veil or gloves. Once the bees have been removed, the honey supers can be removed from the colonies with ease.

This beekeeper is using forced air to blow bees out of a super of ripe honey.

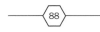

### Homemade bee escapes

A variety of homemade bee escapes have been devised, and they are just as satisfactory as the factory-made metal escapes. The problem with all bee escapes is that the holes through which the bees move may become plugged with dead bees if there is overheating as a result of a lack of ventilation. For this reason, most beekeepers who build their own escapes use two escape holes instead of one.

### Bee repellents

Several chemicals will repel honey bees and can be used to drive them off combs of honey at harvest time. Only two of these substances, however, are acceptable to the Environmental Protection Agency. One is benzaldehyde, better known as artificial almond extract, which is used by bakers to flavor almond cookies; the odor is pleasant, and the chemical is clearly nontoxic. The second chemical is butric anhydride, sold under the name of Bee-Go. It is a well-known laboratory compound commonly called "stink." There is no question that it is the most effective of the bee repellents, but many beekeepers refuse to use it because its odor lingers for days in the clothing and equipment of the user; still, it is widely used. A perfumed butric anhydride, sold under the name Bee Robber, has been made and it is equally satisfactory as the unperfumed material in repelling and driving bees off combs.

Repellents are used by placing them on an absorbent cloth pad tacked onto a 2-inch-deep rim that is the same size as the super from which the bees are to be driven. When using a repellent you should always start the bees downward, off the combs, with smoke, before putting the pads in place. Too much repellent, or warm days that cause it to evaporate rapidly, will overwhelm and confuse the bees. However, with experience you will learn that repellents can be an effective method of harvesting honey.

### Forced air

The use of forced air to blow bees out of honey supers has become increasingly popular in the past few years, especially with some of the larger commercial beekeepers. Since elaborate equipment and some type of power supply is needed, the method is not too practical for the beekeeper with only a few colonies. Still, some beekeepers have built homemade blowers that work quite well. The physical act of blowing the bees out of the supers apparently does them no harm.

### Brushing and shaking bees

The oldest method of removing combs of honey from a colony is to remove them one at a time, after having smoked the super, and to shake and brush the bees off the combs. This technique works well enough if you have only a few supers of combs to remove. However, bees that are brushed and shaken can become quite angry, and you'll need to work with haste. The chief advantage of this method is that no special equipment is needed. A brush of grass works quite well. Shaking and brushing bees involves more exposure of the combs of honey than any other technique. It is therefore quite easy to stimulate robbing at the time, and special care should be exercised to avoid this.

## EXTRACTING

Extracting is the process of removing liquid honey from the comb. The main reason that honey is extracted is so the comb, which is costly both for bee-keepers and the bees to produce, can be reused. Insofar as the beekeeper is concerned, the object should be to remove the honey and retain as much of its quality as possible. All too frequently, however, the honey is either improperly extracted or damaged in the extracting process. The major problems are incorporating too much air, which results in foam on the top of the final package, and overheating the honey before it is bottled.

The extracting process involves three basic steps: uncapping the combs of honey; placing the uncapped combs in the centrifugal-force machine (extractor) to remove the honey; and straining the honey to remove any bits of wax or other extraneous material that might be accidentally introduced into it. The extracting process can be speeded up considerably if the honey is warmed before it is removed from the comb. Some beekeepers who have only a few colonies of bees extract the honey immediately after removing it from the hive, thus taking advantage of the higher hive temperature to keep the honey warm. Commercial beekeepers often place supers of honey in a heated room, a room usually kept at about 95°F. It is also possible to force air through supers, both to remove excess moisture and to warm the honey.

Several types of uncapping knives and machines are available. A beginning beekeeper, with only a hive or two, will be satisfied to use a so-called *cold knife*. This resembles a butcher knife, with a fairly heavy steel blade. The knife is placed in hot water so the blade is warmed prior to cutting the wax cappings from the comb. Usually two knives are used; one is heating while the second one is used to uncap. Beekeepers with more colonies may wish to use electric- or steam-heated knives. Some commercial beekeepers use power uncappers, which remove the cappings from many combs per minute.

As is the case with uncapping methods, there is great variation in the size and type of extractors available. The beginner will find that a two- or three-frame, nonreversible extractor will suffice; however, extractors are available that hold as many as 100 or more combs.

Since equipment for extracting can be expensive, it is often advisable for a beginning beekeeper to cooperate with other beekeepers, or to seek out a commercial beekeeper who will extract the honey at a rate of so many cents a pound. This has the added advantage of acquainting the beginner with the various types of uncapping knives and extractors on the market, together with their advantages and disadvantages. Often, you may buy secondhand extractors and uncapping knives at the same time you purchase secondhand beehives.

### Cappings

The wax cappings that are cut from a comb to be extracted usually contain quite a bit of honey. This honey can be salvaged, but not without some difficulty. Cappings usually retain honey, which can be removed only after they have been crushed and broken.

Perhaps the easiest way to remove honey from cappings is to place them in a wooden or metal container with a coarse screen bottom and to allow them to drain for a day or two. Some beekeepers place such containers in a special warming oven or room, since warming the cappings speeds up the draining process. If the cappings are broken with a knife or trowel, they will drain reasonably well.

Cappings can also be placed in an extractor, equipped with special baskets and the honey centrifuged out in much the same way it is removed from a comb. However, this is a sticky, messy process; allowing

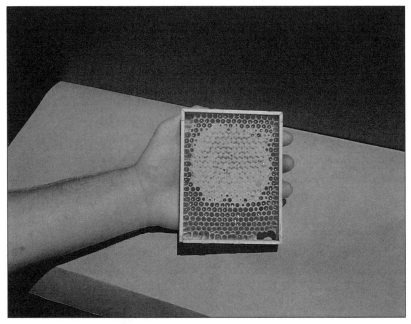

*On this section of honey only those cells in the center have been capped, indicating the honey is not yet ripe, or that the nectar flow ended before the section was finished.*

the cappings to drain is easier, even though it takes a longer period of time.

Commercial beekeepers have a variety of ways to remove the honey from cappings. One old method involves placing the partially drained cappings in a wax press and pressing the honey out. More recently, a continuous centrifuge has been developed that can remove the honey from cappings; however, this is a costly machine used only by beekeepers with many colonies.

A few beekeepers, who have apiaries in remote locations where there are no other bees, sometimes use such a site to allow the bee to rob the cappings, thus salvaging honey and at the same time making it easier to handle the cappings. Cappings that have been robbed, and are not sticky with honey, may be shoveled or handled much as one would treat dry sawdust.

Cappings wax is lighter in color than is wax rendered from old combs because the cappings are at most only moderately travel-stained

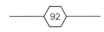

and contain little or no pollen or propolis. For this reason, cappings wax usually fetches a premium price in the market. It is therefore advisable to keep cappings wax separate from old comb wax when the wax is rendered or sold.

## WHOLESALING HONEY

If you produce more honey than you can use or sell in the immediate vicinity, you may decide to package it for the wholesale trade. The common bulk honey containers are the 60-pound metal can or plastic bucket and the 50-gallon drum; however, the 60-pound containers are not so popular with large honey packers today. Some honey packers pay less for honey in 60-pound cans because more labor is involved in handling the smaller container.

Beekeepers who produce only a few drums a year find they do not necessarily need special equipment to handle these large containers. If the honey in the drums is allowed to crystallize, the drums can be tipped on their sides onto an old tire and rolled without danger of spilling the honey. Most honeys crystallize rapidly in the fall. Crystallization can be encouraged by stirring some honey that is already partially crystallized into the drum.

Honey packaged in large cans or drums can ferment if it is not pasteurized or if the moisture level is too high. Few beekeepers pasteurize the honey they sell to the wholesale trade. They do, however, attempt to extract only honey with the proper moisture content. Storing the honey in an unheated warehouse in the winter, at a temperature well below 50°F. (10°C), will protect the honey from fermentation. Honey sold in the wholesale trade should be strained so as to remove all excess wax particles.

## SMALL-SCALE PROCESSING OF LIQUID HONEY FOR MARKET

The beekeeper who produces only a small quantity of honey is at a disadvantage in packing. The large honey packer is able to blend to suit the taste of a market. A packer may also blend honey so as to balance the moisture content, or, if necessary, use a vacuum pan to reduce the moisture content of high-moisture honey. Most large packers of honey filter it, which gives it a distinct sparkle and also extends the shelf life. While filtration has these advantages, we know, too, that it removes the pollen and a certain amount of the flavor from the honey.

Small producers should do the best job possible to sell a product that will result in repeat sales. In many areas of the country it may be advantageous to buy a small quantity of honey and blend it with that which is being packed for the local market. When a honey with a distinct flavor is packed, a special descriptive label, or a second label, can be used to advantage.

Since the small-scale beekeeper has little control over the moisture content of the honey, it is best to remove only honey that has been fully ripened by the bees. It is possible to remove moisture from honey still in the comb by placing it in a heated room and directing a current of warm air over the combs. In fact, in a well-made ventilated room, it may be possible to remove as much as 1 percent moisture from honey in the comb in 24 hours. However, it is almost impossible for the small beekeeper to remove moisture from honey once it has been extracted from the comb.

## BOTTLING AND LABELING

The standard retail packages in which honey is sold are the ½-, 1-, and 2-pound jars and the 5-pound jar or plastic tub. Liquid honey prepared for the retail trade should be strained or be as clean as honey strained through an 80-mesh screen. Honey that has been heated and allowed to settle slowly, or that has been baffled, will usually be as clean as that which is strained.

To clarify honey with a baffle involves constructing a tank with two barriers a few inches apart. The first barrier is raised off the floor of the tank two or three inches so that honey may flow under, up between, and over the top of the second of the two barriers. The second barrier is two or three inches away from the first barrier and is fixed firmly to the bottom of the tank. Since any debris found in honey, such as bits of wax or comb, floats slowly to the top, the honey on the bottom of the tank is clear and clean. Some beekeepers use two or three baffles in a tank. How well a baffle tank works is a function of time and temperature. At room temperature, a baffle tank works very slowly and two to three days may be needed to clarify the honey. Honey should not be heated to more than 90°F for baffling, but at this temperature the honey will clarify in a day or less. Baffle tanks may be 12 to 50 or more inches deep but shallow baffle tanks work best as the debris has less distance to reach the surface.

The honey should be heated to 140°F (60°C) for 30 minutes, or 160°F (71°C) for 1 minute, or some intermediate combination to pasteurize it and to prevent fermentation. Honey packed in the jar and capped while it is still hot will have a longer shelf life (will not granulate so rapidly) than honey that has been packed cold.

Most beekeepers who pack their own honey use a jacketed hot-water tank heated with electricity or gas. Several models are available from the bee supply companies. Too often the honey is overheated, usually because it is kept at a high temperature for too long before being packed.

In commercial packing plants, a machine for removing dust from new glass jars is used before the jars are filled with honey. Even jars just received from the factory may contain dust, which can cause premature granulation. For this reason the beekeeper should make some provision to clean the jars before packing the honey in them.

Labels for honey jars are available from bee supply companies. Unfortunately, all too often the label is designed to sell to the beekeeper, not for the beekeeper to sell honey to the consumer. Most beekeepers like to see a picture of a bee or a beehive on their honey label; most consumers think of bees as just another insect, and so the picture of a bee is not that appealing to them.

Certain colors complement honey more than others; which colors should be used on the label depends upon the color of the honey. Most of these questions concerning marketing and the factors that affect the sale of food products have been carefully researched. The marketing-minded beekeeper may care to pursue this subject in greater detail.

## ROADSIDE STANDS

Some beekeepers have used roadside stands effectively to sell all or part of their honey crop. The chief advantage is that the beekeeper sells the honey at the higher, retail-market price. The major disadvantage appears to be that customers may talk so long, or ask so many questions about bees, that the beekeeper loses too much time when making a sale.

Self-service honey stands are popular with many beekeepers; they are equipped with a box, open or with a sealed cover, into which the customer deposits the money. In areas of high population density, thievery is sometimes a problem. At the same time, a roadside stand is effective only in a well-populated area or where there is heavy traffic on the road.

Roadside stands, servicing of garden stores and vegetable stands, the mail-order trade, and wholesaling are all potential markets through which you can sell honey. I have known beekeepers who have done well in each of these sales areas.

## VARIATION IN HONEY

Just as flowers vary in size, color, shape, and odor, so the nectars they produce vary. Bees use all these factors for orientation as they fly from one flower to another in the field. We benefit from this great variation and harvest honey with many colors and flavors. This has both advantages and disadvantages for the beekeeper. Those who understand these variations will enjoy tasting different honeys. The customer who buys only one or two jars of honey a year, however, can be confused when the second jar of honey does not taste like the first.

You cannot expect the customer to know everything about a product. For this reason it is often advisable to label the jar with the type of honey it contains. Some beekeepers have a second label printed with descriptive information; this label is placed on the jar opposite the first one.

Then, too, there are probably certain honeys that should not be placed on the general market simply because they are too strong and not yet known or favored by the average consumer. Often, certain of the stronger-flavored honeys are better appreciated if they are blended with a milder honey. The flavor of the strong honey will still dominate but is not so harsh as to be objectionable. (Examples of strong-flavored honeys that benefit from dilution with milder honeys are buckwheat and goldenrod.) Often, in their enthusiasm to produce and market a certain type of honey, beekeepers forget that the public has little or no knowledge of honey. In general, the American public prefers a light-colored, mild-flavored honey. The successful seller of honey must cater to these tastes.

## NUTRITIONAL LABELING

In 1990, the United States Congress passed the Nutritional Labeling and

Education Act, which was signed into law by the president. This requires the nutritional labeling of most foods (except for meat and poultry, which is overseen by the United States Department of Agriculture). The portions having to do with health claims were effective in 1993 and the rest took effect in May 1994. The legislation has some virtue in that terms such as "light," "low-fat," and "high-fiber" are now defined and have a real meaning. However, there is a question in the minds of many people if the legislation should be extended to a luxury product such as honey. Small businesses that have food sales of less than $50,000 per year are exempted, at least for the present. Regulations prepared under the new act are enforced by the Pure Food and Drug Administration, which is part of the Department of Health and Human Services.

---
⬡6⬡
---

# FALL MANAGEMENT

IN MANY PARTS OF THE UNITED STATES AND CANADA, GOLDEN-rod and aster, especially goldenrod, are major sources of nectar in the fall. There are numerous species of goldenrod that are native American plants, and some are found in all states. Over much of its range, goldenrod is present in sufficient quantity that bees may store large amounts of honey from it for winter. Goldenrod is a fairly dark honey, and one of the best honeys available for the bakery trade; however, it is not good winter food for bees because it contains too much protein and other materials that accumulate as fecal matter in winter bees. This is no problem if the bees take frequent flights to void feces, but it can cause trouble if the bees are confined for long periods of time. This point is discussed more fully below, and you must take this fact of nature into account when formulating your fall management scheme.

Soon after the first of August is the time you should begin to think about the general condition of your colonies. A good colony of bees should have a young, vigorous queen that will lay eggs late in the fall so as to have as many young bees in the winter cluster as possible. A young queen is also an advantage in the spring, as such a queen will start brood rearing earlier in the year and produce a more populous colony by the time of the spring honey flow. For these two reasons it is often said the beekeeper's year begins on August 1st and that, where annual requeening is practiced, it should be done at about that time.

## SWARMING AND FALL MANAGEMENT

About 20 percent of colonies swarm in the fall. This figure though, was obtained as a result of research in the vicinity of Ithaca, New York, and may not be correct elsewhere. You need not worry too much about providing ample room for the brood nest after about the first of July; however, ample room should be made available for honey storage.

I myself prefer to place queen excluders on colonies above a single brood-nest super sometime after about July 8th in New York State, and earlier further north. Since the last swarming in my area occurs around July 15th there are almost no queen cells built after about July 8th. Many beekeepers argue against using queen excluders, but excluders make fall management easier. Since crowding the queen into a single super after July 8th seldom precipitates swarming, there is little danger in this regard. In fact, during the first two weeks after the queen is placed in the bottom super, congestion is usually relieved; the bottom super is typically empty and contains little or no brood, honey, or pollen at this time of year. It has been said that queen excluders hinder the movement of bees within the colony and interfere with ventilation of the hive, but there is no hard data to back up these statements or to prove that queen excluders have an adverse effect on honey production.

The chief advantage of using a queen excluder above a single brood-nest super is that the bees will fill the second super—the one immediately above the brood nest—with honey. In the North, a colony of bees needs 60 to 70 pounds of honey to winter successfully. The preferred system of wintering bees involves using two supers, and it is absolutely essential that one of these supers is packed full of honey. If a queen excluder is not used, the queen will often continue to use at least a part of the second super for brood rearing purposes. This means the beekeeper must rearrange the combs in the supers in the fall, a job that, while not impossible, is much easier left to the bees.

A second advantage of a queen excluder is that one need not worry about having brood in combs about to be extracted. Where bee escapes are used, excluders are also an advantage since the brood is below it and the bee escapes are merely substituted for the excluders.

In most of the northern states, fall honey flows are more erratic than spring honey flows. Goldenrod does not yield nectar every year or in every location. When goldenrod does yield, however, crops of 50 to over 100 pounds per colony are not unusual.

I once thought I had devised a perfect system for the management of bees in the southern tier of New York State. The aim was to make a maximum fall crop, which is the chief honey flow in this area. I split my over-wintered colonies and requeened the queenless halves, or allowed them to requeen themselves, in late April. This circumvented the swarming problem, since the newly divided colonies were too weak to swarm in May and June. Then I rotated the positions of the colonies in the apiary in June and July to equalize their strength. By August 1st the colonies were usually in three or four supers and had a small reserve of honey. On about August 1st I drove the queens into the bottom super using a repellent and added an excluder above the first super. The colonies were then given an additional super or two.

The goldenrod flow in the North can start as early as August 1st or as late as September 10th. Occasionally, though, there is no fall honey flow at all, and these are the times when my "perfect" system fails me.

In a good year, the goldenrod will be frost-killed in late September, and this may be followed by a honey flow from asters. When it is time to remove the honey, using the above system of management, it is only necessary to select those colonies that are in the best condition for wintering. The queen excluders are removed and the second super, which should weigh 60 to 70 pounds, is left for the winter food chamber. All the supers above this one are removed and extracted. The remaining colonies may be killed and the entire crop removed. The honey yield in a good year, based on the spring count, will usually be above 200 pounds, but only in those years when there is a good goldenrod honey flow. This system will work well in any area in the country where the chief honey flow is in the late summer or early fall but is obviously not suitable everywhere.

## REQUEENING

A young queen lays more eggs, maintains a more compact brood pattern, has a stronger colony that is more resistant to stress-related diseases, lays eggs later in the fall and earlier in the spring, and (finally, and perhaps most importantly) produces more of the secretions that are vital to maintaining social order in the colony. For this last reason, swarming is much less of a problem when a young queen is present in a colony. Annual requeening of colonies is a practice recommended in most books on bees. It is routinely practiced by some commercial beekeepers; other beekeepers try to watch their colonies more closely and attempt to requeen only those that have failing queens.

When annual requeening is done, it is probably best to do so around August 1st. September requeening may be satisfactory, but not all colonies will accept a new queen. If the requeening is done in early August, then it may be possible to requeen those colonies in which it first fails.

There are several methods of requeening, some easier and more certain than others. One common practice is to find the old queen and kill her, placing a queen cage with the young queen in the brood nest to be released by the bees in a day or two. How well this strategy works depends upon a number of factors. If there is a honey flow in progress, the queen will be more readily accepted by the other bees, though even this is not always true.

A preferred method of requeening is to introduce a young queen into a nucleus colony containing one frame of brood and two or three frames of bees about mid-July. A young queen is almost always accepted under such circumstances. Around August 1st the queen in the old colony may be found and killed. A single sheet of newspaper is then placed above the old queen's brood nest and the nucleus colony placed above the newspaper. The honey supers are placed above this, but if there are too many bees in them, they should be shaken out, or a second sheet of newspaper placed between the nucleus and the honey supers. By the time the bees have chewed away the newspaper, the colony odors will be the same and the young queen will be accepted. If a queen excluder is to be placed on the colony, this should be delayed for a week or two, at which time the young queen may be successfully driven into the lower brood chamber.

It is good beekeeping practice to keep a few small colonies in reserve for emergency requeening. Whenever two colonies are combined, the safest and easiest method is to use the single sheet of newspaper; most beekeepers cut a few small slash lines in the paper to speed up its removal by the bees, but this is not really necessary.

## THE QUALITY OF FALL HONEY AS BEE FOOD

In the winter, honey bees cluster. Not only do they fill the spaces between the combs, but many crawl into cells. The outer shell of this cluster resembles a ball in shape, and, like a ball, the outer surface is a compact mass (of bees) while the inside is hollow. A cross section of what a winter cluster might look like within a colony may be seen in a glass-walled observation hive on a cold fall or spring day if the hive is in a cool room.

Bees in the center of the cluster warm it by eating honey and physically moving to generate heat. Large quantities of honey are necessary to keep the colony alive throughout the winter. Honey bees do not defecate within the hive under ordinary circumstances; in fact, if they do so, social order usually breaks down and the colony dies.

Since bees consume large quantities of honey in the winter and waste products accumulate in the lower digestive tract as a result, it is important that either the food be as free of indigestible matter as possible, or that the bees have frequent flights to void fecal matter.

Today, only a few beekeepers winter their bees in cellars or temperature-controlled buildings, but those who do feed their colonies sugar syrup in the late fall. Beekeepers who live in the more northern parts of the Northeast, but who winter their bees outdoors, can also feed the colonies 10 or 20 pounds of sugar syrup in the fall, or they can attempt to use only high-quality honey for winter food.

As mentioned earlier, some honeys have a tendency to granulate more rapidly than others. Aster honey makes very poor winter food because it granulates so hard that it is difficult for the bees to remove it

*The colonies in New York State are being loaded on a truck to be sent to Florida in the fall.*

from the cells in the comb. Thus, the question of winter food is more important in some regions than in others. It is important that you understand your local situation to take the steps necessary for the successful wintering of your colonies.

## FALL DRUG FEEDING

Many beekeepers do not care to use drugs to protect their bees from disease. I have usually agreed with this position. However, varroa and tracheal mites have complicated the picture, and I now recommend fall medication, which will do much to aid in colony survival over the winter. This is true because colonies with multiple diseases are under a greater stress and are more likely to die than colonies that have to cope with only one or two diseases. (For more details, see Chapter 8.)

## ⬡7⬡
# WINTERING HONEY BEES

I N THE NORTHERN UNITED STATES, HONEY BEES SHOULD BE given some special protection during the winter months. While a colony can survive without special attention, and many do, the general condition of a colony will be greatly improved if it is given some packing. Cold weather is not a problem for honey bees; their efficient clustering system is designed to protect them against great extremes of cold. However, in the process of eating honey, bees give off great quantities of water. It is important to get rid of this water so that it does not condense within the hive. At the same time, bees consuming honey accumulate fecal matter, which they must void outside of the hive if the colony is to remain in good condition. In the case of old bees, it is far better that they be encouraged to fly out of the hive in the winter to void feces, and not return, than it is that they remain in the hive and void fecal matter there. The use of winter packing is designed to assist the bees in these two problems of ridding the colony of excess moisture and of encouraging winter flight as much as possible.

## WEIGHING COLONIES

Unfortunately, only a few beekeepers weigh their colonies in the fall, even though it is the only accurate way to determine how much food a colony has stored for winter. Most beekeepers merely lift their colonies from one end to check on winter stores; this is not a satisfactory method of checking the quantity of winter food and should be discouraged. Buying a pair of scales for weighing colonies is well worth the investment. A difference of only a few pounds can be important.

A two-story (two full-depth supers) colony in the North with an ordinary bottomboard and cover, combs, honey, and bees should weigh 130 pounds to winter satisfactorily. If the colony weighs less than this, it should be fed. Feeding should be done shortly after the goldenrod is killed by cold weather in the fall. By feeding at this time of the year, the bees have time to arrange their winter stores in the manner they prefer.

There are various methods for weighing bees, but for one person a two-legged stand is probably the most satisfactory. A set of scales mounted on a pole for weighing by two people works rapidly. Once a colony has been weighed, the weights should be written on the cover so you'll know at a glance exactly how much syrup to feed.

## FALL FEEDING

When bees store nectar as honey, they remove moisture from it. Because bees will also remove water from sugar syrup that is fed for winter, it should be more concentrated than that which is used for spring feeding. In the fall, the syrup is made with two parts sugar to one part water; in the spring, the mixture is made one to one by weight or volume.

Bees cannot digest all of the sugars humans can. This is seldom a problem, as most beekeepers feed their bees only sucrose (ordinary table sugar) or isomerose. If some other sugar is used, the literature should be checked to make sure the bees can digest it. Waste sugar, or sugar that is salvaged in candy plants, etc., is sometimes fed to bees. This is better used as spring food, as it may contain some indigestible matter. Only a high-quality food, that is, one which contains only sucrose or isomerose, should be given to bees in the fall.

There are many ways to feed sugar to bees: pails, division board feeders, entrance feeders, pouring syrup into empty combs, pan-feeding above or below the brood nest, dry-sugar feeding, and mass feeding outside of the hive. Some of these methods are better than others. (See "Spring feeding" in Chapter 3.)

## METHODS OF PACKING BEES

In the northern states, a variety of methods have been used to pack bees for winter. (The term "pack" is really a misnomer; it dates from the time when bees were "packed" with sawdust or straw in a refrigerator-type packing box. The theory at the time was that bees needed assistance to conserve heat; we now know that this is not the most important consideration.) Winter preparation may or may not involve placing a protective wrapper around the colony, depending upon the severity of the winters in the region where you live.

The most popular and successful winter wrapping material is black building paper. The lighter the weight of the paper, the better. Many beekeepers use slater's felt for winter wrapping, but this is too heavy. For the most successful winter pack, the paper should be waterproof, but "breathable" enough to allow some slight movement of moisture-laden air through the paper. Under no circumstances should plastic be used to wrap colonies for winter, as it does not allow moisture to escape.

Several years ago, wooden packing cases, into which colonies were placed, were commonplace. A few beekeepers have even constructed metal packing cases. Research on the winter survival of honey bee colonies, however, indicates heavy winter packing is not helpful. The winter cluster must be able to move to new stores, and the bees within the hive must be able to rid themselves of accumulated fecal matter. These two factors are more important than anything else, insofar as the successful wintering of bees is concerned.

*Colonies of honey bees given winter protection produce more brood earlier in the year. The steps in wrapping colonies in black, water-resistant building paper are illustrated here. The holes in the colony's inner covers are left open and the top is covered with wheat straw which absorbs moisture. The rounded top of the winter pack sheds rain and snow. The wrap is tied in place with binder's twine.*

### The tarpaper wrap

The most efficient method of packing bees is to wrap the colonies on hive stands that can accommodate two to four colonies. Hive stands built for two colonies are most common; when more than this number of colonies is packed in a group, there will be too much drifting (when bees accidently enter a hive not their own) after the bees are packed in the fall and before they are unpacked in the spring. However, this is not considered to be a serious problem by many beekeepers.

Only a single layer of paper, which is usually sold in 3-foot-wide rolls, is needed for the wrap. For packing two standard 10-frame, two-story hives, a piece 9 feet 4 inches long will overlap 5 or 6 inches when wrapped around the two hives. No packing or insulation material should be used under the tarpaper on the sides of the colonies. Place a material that absorbs moisture, preferably wheat straw, 8 to 10 inches high on top of

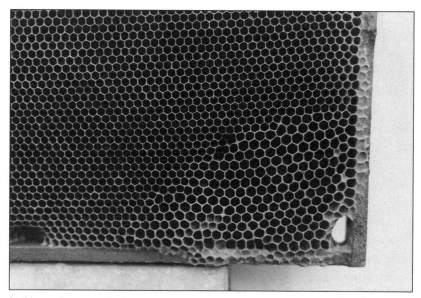

*In this comb we see the larger drone cells in the lower right-hand corner. It is most likely that this corner of the comb was chewed out by a nest-making mouse. The bees rebuilt the comb after the mouse was driven from the hive.*

the colony's innercovers. If the holes in the innercovers are left open, there will be a good escape passage for moisture-laden air.

At the point where the wrapping paper overlaps, weave two nails into the paper to hold it in place. Nails woven into the paper are the easiest to use to hold the top corners of the pack down. Use a single piece of string, usually heavy binder twine, to tie the paper in place.

The effectiveness of the pack is best judged in the spring. The colony should be dry at that time. If any part of the interior is wet, then the pack was too tight. In more humid areas it may be advisable to put nail holes in the side of the pack to allow moisture-laden air to escape.

## MICE IN BEE HIVES

Mice can be very destructive to beekeeping equipment. Not only do they destroy much stored equipment each year, but in the fall mice may invade and overwinter in active colonies. After the winter cluster is formed the bees abandon a large portion of the hive. The bees in a winter cluster cannot move from the cluster to protect all the space in the hive while the temperature remains cold. The mice move into the hive at that time and chew out an area in the comb, and surround their nests with leaves and other insulating material. This nest lining also prevents the bees from attacking and driving the mice out of the hive when the weather warms sufficiently for the bees to move. The mice apparently learn to remain inactive at the time when the colony is active. In the spring a female mouse may raise a litter of young before moving out of the hive.

Many beekeepers reduce the size of their colony entrances in the fall with wooden or metal mouse guards, which will usually work reasonably well to exclude mice. However, these can be dangerous gadgets. There are often long periods of time during a harsh winter when a number of bees may die, fall to the bottom of the hive, block the entrance, and thus cause the colony to suffocate. If a colony entrance is to be reduced for this or any other reason in the fall, a second entrance is recommended. This is best made by drilling a ¾- or 1-inch diameter hole just under the hand hold of the top super. It is suggested that the upper entrance be made under the hand hold so that you will not cover the hole with your hand, and possibly be stung when removing the super.

## SNOW AND SNOWBANKS

Whereas we have written about the importance of winter flights, it is a fact that colonies buried in a snowbank for a month or more fare quite well even though the bees can have no flight. Apparently, a colony covered with snow is insulated and does not suffer from the extremes of temperature that have an adverse effect. Our experience in the northern states is that there is no need to dig out or expose a colony covered with snow.

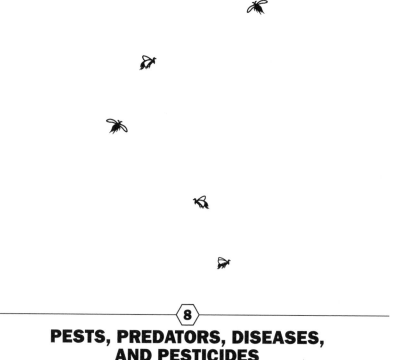

---

⟨8⟩

# PESTS, PREDATORS, DISEASES,
# AND PESTICIDES

THREE NEW DISEASES OF HONEY BEES HAVE BEEN accidently introduced into the United States in recent years (chalkbrood, tracheal, and varroa mites). Adding to these problems is the fact that many state departments of agriculture, which are or have been responsible for honey bee disease detection and control, have cut or eliminated the amount of money used for this purpose because of the pressure to use tax money for other programs. The federal government usually plays only an advisory role as concerns bee diseases; however, it does maintain a laboratory where the organisms causing the diseases may be identified when questions arise. In most states it is up to you, the beekeeper, to identify and treat the diseases that may otherwise kill your colonies.

## NATURAL METHODS OF BEE DISEASE CONTROL

Honey bees in a hive are packed closely together with their brood and food. Under these circumstances one would expect that contagious diseases would spread rapidly, and sometimes they do. However, honey bees have a number of natural physical and chemical defense systems that protect them, their food, and their homes against attack and destruction.

One of the most important features of hive life is the natural cleanliness that bees exhibit. Dead and sick bees, as well as foreign objects, are carried to the hive entrance, where the housecleaning bees take flight and usually deposit these objects 50 to 100 or more feet away from the hive where they will not be a source of reinfection. One may demonstrate this by introducing dead bees, or foreign objects such as bits of grass, into the top of a glass-walled observation hive and then watching the rapidity with which this refuse is picked up and carried out of the hive by house bees. Often more than one bee will participate in the removal of an object. It is important that hive entrances be kept clear of grass and debris so that bees carrying debris may take flight easily.

Honey bees also do a great deal of grooming, both of themselves and other bees, and it is in this manner that many pests and parasites are kept under control. Grooming is especially important in protecting against varroa disease, which is discussed more fully later in the chapter.

Honey has several properties that protect it against attack by microbes. First of all, honey is an acidic food, with an average pH of about 3.9. Most bacteria and their relatives cannot live in such an acid environment. Honey also has a high osmotic pressure. *Osmosis* is the process whereby water passes through a semipermeable membrane, such as the cell wall of an organism, thus equalizing conditions on both sides. When bacteria are introduced into a medium such as honey, water passes out of their cells and they dry up and die because of this high osmotic pressure, which the bacteria can neither control nor resist. Some microbes may remain alive in the spore or resting stage in honey but cannot grow or multiply there.

When bees are ripening honey, through lowering its moisture content they also add an enzyme that attacks a small amount of the sugar glucose that is present, converting it into gluconic acid and hydrogen peroxide. The gluconic acid gives honey its low pH. Hydrogen peroxide ($H_2O_2$) is a well-known bactericide and is sold over the counter in drug stores. It is used to wash and cleanse wounds and to disinfect instruments and laboratory benches. The glucose oxidase system works only when honey has a moisture content of more than about 19 percent and thus gives protection to the honey as it is being ripened and when it is diluted for larval feeding. Hydrogen peroxide is not a very stable compound and soon breaks down into water and free oxygen.

Pollen also has special mechanisms that protect it. Honey is often added to pollen, especially dry pollen, to make it sticky so that it will remain in a bee's pollen basket. In this manner, the honey may give the pollen some protection. However, when it is packed into a cell, *Pseudomonas* bacteria consume a small amount of the honey and pollen and in the process use up the oxygen that is present. This allows *Lactobacillus* bacteria, which are not active when oxygen is present, to grow, and when they do, they produce lactic acid, which is a natural preservative and protects the pollen. Bees never fill cells containing pollen to more than about 80 percent of their capacity. If the pollen is to be consumed immediately the cells are left uncovered, but if it is to be stored for a longer period of time, the remaining 20 percent of the cell is covered with honey, which serves to protect the pollen on the surface. While stored pollen does deteriorate slowly, its quality remains high for several months because of this natural chemical process.

Honey bees also collect *propolis*, the name we give the gums and resins they gather, especially from poplar and pine trees. Propolis is used to fill cracks and crevices where bacteria, mold, and even insects may hide and breed, thus eliminating these sites. It is also used to varnish any and all rough spots on wood and the combs. We use carefully planed wood to make frames and hive interiors to reduce the amount of propolis bees can collect. Propolis is a nuisance for beekeepers because it sticks to their fingers, hive tools, and clothing.

All of these natural, physical, and chemical controls are important in hive life. In selecting bees that may be resistant to one or more diseases, we

may emphasize or encourage some of these factors, especially grooming and hive cleanliness.

## CLIMATE CONTROL INSIDE THE BEE HIVE

Honey bees maintain a high brood-rearing temperature of about 92° to 96° F (33°-35°C). However, it is the temperature in the compact brood nest that is controlled, not the temperature of the whole of the inside of the hive. If colonies have dry bottomboards they are better able to maintain this temperature. If the bottomboards are wet, however, the bees will attempt to dry them, and the resulting evaporation of water is a cooling process that may affect the whole hive interior. It is recommended that colonies be kept on some kind of hive stand, 6 to 10 inches high, with good air circulation underneath. Keeping grass cut around hives will also help to keep hives dry. In the southern states, beekeepers usually paint their hives white to protect them against overheating. In the north, hives are often painted with darker paints that will absorb the sun's heat and presumably help to keep the hives warm and dry.

## PESTS, PREDATORS, AND DISEASES

In the paragraphs that follow, the most serious of the honey bee diseases are discussed, together with control measures. We have good control methods for most of these problems, but early detection is also important. Successfully attacking a disease includes diagnosing the problem before the colony becomes severely weakened and while it still has a sufficient number of bees to survive.

### Varroa mites

On September 26, 1987, *Varroa jacobsoni*, a mite that is a parasite of the small Asian honey bee, was found for the first time in the United States in Wisconsin, in a colony belonging to a migratory beekeeper from Florida. A search for the mites was made immediately in Florida, where they were discovered only a few days later. Soon after that, the mites were found in migratory bees in New York State, and it was understood that the mites were already widespread in the United States, and that their further spread could not be stopped. Varroa mites cause the most serious of all of the known diseases of European honey bees.

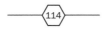

The mites were probably introduced together with queen honey bees from South America that were illegally brought into this country. Varroa mites had been identified many years earlier in Europe, and fortunately we had the benefit of previous research when they were found in this country. Cornell University had a project on varroa in Brazil from 1980 through 1986 that also provided us with much information concerning the mite's biology and control.

The life history of *Varroa jacobsoni* is well-known. Mated female mites that are about to produce eggs move into drone and worker cells containing larvae just before the cells are capped. Drone cells are preferred. The mites go to the bottoms of the cells, where they immerse themselves and feed on the residual royal jelly (larval food) that is there. When they and the honey bee larvae have finished this food they start to produce eggs that soon hatch. The young varroa, as well as the old female, pierce the integument of the honey bee larvae, now turned pupa, and feed on its blood. If there are many varroa present, the bee will die. If there are only a few varroa the bee may continue to develop, but when it emerges from its cell it usually has a shorter life span or is somehow maimed and has under-developed wings and/or legs. The young varroa then mate inside the cell, and the males remain there and die. The young females emerge from the cells, attach themselves to a worker bee, and burrow under the bee's abdominal segments, on either side of the wax glands, where they feed on the adult's blood. They take no other food. Sometime after they are engorged, they leave the bee and the cycle is repeated.

A great many chemicals have been tested in Europe for varroa control even before the mites were discovered in the United States. We have since done much testing in this country. Several of these compounds are reasonably good, being nontoxic to honey bees and highly toxic to mites. It is a curious fact that many chemicals are active against one form of life and innocuous to another. We can expect that in the future, we will be forced to change the chemicals that we use for varroa control since mites are notorious for the rapidity with which they can build up resistance to pesticides.

The Asian honey bees that are the native host for varroa protect themselves through grooming. They bite and mutilate the mites and remove them from the hive. This simple control mechanism is adequate to give the bees

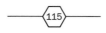

good control over the mites and, while they are always present, their numbers never become very high in Asian honey bee colonies. Africanized bees in Brazil protect themselves in the same manner. Again, while varroa mites are found in every hive of Africanized honey bees where they are searched for in Brazil, the Brazilian beekeepers never treat their colonies for varroa or worry about the mites being a menace.

A very small number of colonies of European honey bees that resist mites through grooming have been found in the United States and Europe. These are being examined for other qualities such as honey production and gentleness. It is hoped that from this resistant stock we may develop bees for the future and eventually avoid the necessity of using pesticides to control varroa.

### Tracheal mites

*Acarapis woodi* is a parasitic honey bee mite that was discovered in about 1918 and named in 1921 in Great Britain. It completes its entire life cycle inside the breathing tubes of adult honey bees, especially in the largest of these tubes, which is found in the front part of the thorax. It was found for the first time in the United States in Texas on July 3, 1984. It was widespread in this country by the time it was detected and had been found in Mexico a few years earlier. The United States and Canadian governments had created legislation in 1923 to prevent the further importation of honey bees into this country because of these mites. It is generally agreed that this legislation gave us good protection against them for many years.

*Acarapis woodi* is physically very much like one of the three species of mites that lives externally on honey bees. The external species have been found everywhere the European honey bees are kept. These external mites have been studied carefully. No one has ever been able to determine that they cause any problems in a bee hive.

In the first twenty years of this century an unknown disease ravaged colonies of bees in Great Britain, and most of the bees there died. In 1918, when the tracheal mites were discovered, many people assumed that they were the source of the problem and had caused the loss of colonies. However, since the mites were identified after the worst losses had already taken place, no one had proof.

Soon after these tracheal mites were found in the United States, there were tremendous losses of honey bee colonies in this country, especially in the central and northern states. This caused many people to reexamine the situation and to conclude that these mites were truly the cause of the problem in Great Britain, and that they probably evolved in about 1890 in that country. Around that time, it was thought some of the relatively harmless external mites apparently adapted to living internally inside the breathing tubes of bees, and these individuals developed into a new species.

A great number of chemical controls for tracheal mites have been tested in Europe, but none is satisfactory. It appears that many races of bees in Europe have evolved a natural resistance to these mites since the 1920s, when they were first found on the European continent. This natural resistance is simply the process of the more susceptible bees dying and the more mite-resistant bees surviving.

It was found that fumes from menthol would kill tracheal mites, or at least deter their reproduction. However, for the material to be effective, the temperature must be high enough (above 80°F; 27°C) so that the menthol will evaporate. Fall treatment of colonies, after the honey had been removed, was often recommended. However, these fall treatments do not work too well.

One strain of honey bees from Europe, the Buckfast bee, had been imported and was being sold by a queen breeder in Texas even before tracheal mites were discovered in the United States. This bee has proven to offer good resistance against the mites in most years and is now being widely used. The heavy losses that American beekeepers suffered in the past has also meant that the surviving bees are more resistant to tracheal mites, too. Several queen breeders have incorporated this more resistant stock into their bees.

In Great Britain it is estimated that approcimately 2 percent of colonies still die each winter as a result of tracheal mite infestations. We can expect that losses from these mites will continue in this country at a low level. The best defense against the mites is to take precautions against all of the other diseases that may pose problems, thereby freeing the bees from being weakened by them and leaving them better able to cope with tracheal mites. Our experience is that requeening colonies with queens said to be resistant will prove helpful.

### American foulbrood

American foulbrood has been a problem for American beekeepers for all of

this century. It is a disease caused by a strain of bacteria, *Bacillus larvae,* that infects honey bee larvae and almost invariably kills them in the pupal stage. Before the introduction of varroa and tracheal mites, foulbrood was considered the most serious of all of the honey bee diseases in North America, but now, while it is still a problem, it ranks a distant third. In many states, large sums of money were spent to keep this disease under control so as to have a healthy beekeeping industry that was ready and able to provide the bees that are needed for pollination. In many areas, infection rates were kept in the range of 1 percent, a figure that most beekeepers could live with. However, in recent years, the protection of an agricultural industry using state taxpayer funds has had little support, and conseqently fewer apiary inspections are conducted each year.

There are two problems with American foulbrood that make its control difficult. One is that the bacteria that cause the problem can enter a spore, or resting stage, in which they may remain alive for 50 years or more. A second problem is that the bacteria reduce the dead pupae to a sticky mass that is difficult for the bees to remove from the hive without contaminating other hive parts. It is also easy to contaminate one's hands and hive tools with the disease spores and to transfer them to another hive.

For many years, the treatment of American foulbrood involved the identification and burning of infected colonies, mostly by state apiary inspectors. This was effective and has kept the infection rate low in many areas, so long as states had a number of apiary inspectors. However, the bacteria are also susceptible to antibiotics, and the drug oxytetracycline (trade name: Terramycin) gives good control. It is available from beekeeping supply houses together with directions for its use. Before using it, though, you should determine how much state inspection is available in your area and how much such inspection can be depended upon to aid in control.

### The stress diseases

Four honey bee diseases should be considered as a unit: European foulbrood, sacbrood, chalkbrood, and nosema. The first three affect honey bees in the larval stage; the fourth attacks adults only. All of these diseases may be found in colonies at any time of the year, but they are especially troublesome in the spring, when the colony populations are growing rapidly and outdoor temperatures fluctuate widely; both of these phenomena, as

well as others discussed below, place stress on colonies.

Each of these diseases can be destructive. While they rarely kill a colony, they can keep it in a weakened state for the whole season. It is not uncommon for three or all four of these problems to manifest themselves at the same time. In recent years chalkbrood, which was accidentally introduced into North America in the 1960s, has proven especially troublesome.

Stress can be placed on colonies in many ways. Poor food (honeydew honey, for example), a shortage of pollen, a lack of fresh water, and foul odors (as may occur when mice are present), are all factors. Colonies that have wet bottomboards or that are kept in a damp location may also show problems. Windy locations may both reduce foraging and make hive temperature control more difficult for the bees. Pesticides may suddenly kill some or most of the foraging force, thus reducing the colony's food intake. At night, especially on cool evenings, the foraging force aids in hive temperature control and, if that force is lost, brood may be chilled.

Some of the above stresses can be reduced or eliminated through good management. Hive stands (cinder blocks, stones, old railroad ties) that elevate the colony 4 to 6 inches off the ground are especially helpful in keeping colonies dry. Keeping down the grass and weeds around colonies by mowing, the use of weed killers, or placing cardboard or old packing material around colonies can also prove helpful. It is especially important that the colony entrance not be blocked by high grass. Exposing colonies to full sunlight, especially in the northern states, is advisable; on the other hand, in areas like Arizona it is necessary to shade colonies. In the early spring it is usually advisable to keep colony entrances restricted with a cleat; this is especially true of new colonies started with package bees and colonies with small populations. This will help the bees keep the hive warm. Supers should not be added too early in the spring; neither should the brood nest be split when there is not a sufficient number of bees to care for the brood and the empty space.

As a general rule, requeening is the most effective way to cope with the stress diseases. A young queen produces more eggs and imparts more queen pheromone that presumably stimulates colony activity.

## European foulbrood

European foulbrood is a bacterial disease that affects only larval honey bees. Unlike American foulbrood, the European foulbrood organism *melisso-*

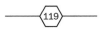

*Grass blocks this colony's entrance indicating the need and value of a hive stand.*

*coccus pluton,* does not form a spore, so it does not pose the great threat that American foulbrood does. Larvae killed by European foulbrood usually die at a younger larval stage than those killed by American foulbrood; the dead larvae are usually found curled or twisted in their cells, whereas those killed by American foulbrood lie perfectly flat. Also, larvae killed by European foulbrood do not have the sticky, ropy consistency of those killed by American foulbrood.

The drug Terramycin gives good control of European foulbrood, but steps should be taken to eliminate the stress that brought about the disease in the first place.

### Sacbrood

Sacbrood is a viral disease that affects only honey bee larvae. The disease got its name because the dead larvae may be lifted from their cells and appear saclike. There are no drugs or medications that have any effect on sacbrood, and the only protection the beekeeper has are the protective measures described above that are taken against the other stress diseases.

*Here are four colonies, elevated on a hive stand, in a good site in an apple orchard.*

### Chalkbrood

Chalkbrood is caused by a fungus that attacks and kills bees in the larval stage. It has long been present in Europe, but when it was introduced here in the 1960s, North American bees had no natural resistance to the disease, and large numbers of colonies were lost or severely weakened. Chalkbrood gets its name from the fact that the dead brood, called "mummies," have a white, chalky appearance; this changes to black when the fungus reaches its reproductive stage. There is no drug that is effective against chalkbrood.

### Nosema

Nosema disease is caused by a microorganism *Nosema apis,* that affects only adult honey bees. The microorganisms invade the cells in the gut of the bee and destroy them, thus upsetting normal digestive and physiological processes. Nosema disease may be found in almost every apiary in almost every part of the country. However, it is usually only in the early spring, when colonies are under stress that the disease manifests itself. The chief symptom is the presence of a large number of weak, crawling bees in front of the colony entrance. Nosema disease may be accompanied by dysentery, which may be brought about either directly by nosema disease or by poor food within the colony. Fumagillin, a drug sold under various trade names, has proved to be fairly effective against nosema disease, but its cost usually prohibits its use by most beekeepers.

A complaint from package bee and queen buyers in the northern states and Canada is that bees are shipped from the southern states infected with nosema. While this is probably true, the same nosema disease causes little or no difficulty in the southern states. Because of the cooler temperatures in the North, increased stress is placed on the bees, and the disease can kill or shorten the lives of a large number of bees in a package shipped north.

### Other microbial diseases

While the four honey bee diseases discussed above are the major ones beekeepers will encounter in the United States, there are several other, lesserknown maladies that affect larval and adult honey bees. These include amoeba, parafoulbrood, and paralysis, to mention only a few you can find listed in the literature.

Generally speaking, these are diseases that cause little loss and for which no special cure is necessary. In part, it is expected that these, too, are diseases that manifest themselves more under stress, and the routine practices recommended above will do much to eliminate them from the apiary.

### Chilled brood

Not infrequently, in the early spring, when the weather is favorable, honey bees will attempt to rear more brood than they can keep warm during a period of adversity. Beekeepers in the northern states have noted that, if a week of inclement weather follows a week of unusually warm weather in the months of April and May, some larvae and/or pupae on the outer edges of the brood nest become chilled and die. If larvae are killed by excessive cold, they are usually removed by house bees within 24 hours and are seldom noticed by the beekeeper. On the other hand, cells containing dead pupae are not uncapped immediately, nor are the pupae removed; in this case the removal process may take several weeks.

In the United States, except for varroa disease, there are no adult bee diseases that kill in the late pupal stage. Thus, when one finds dead pupae within a colony, especially in the early spring, it is almost certain that they died of chilling.

There are no special precautions to be taken to prevent chilled brood except to keep the entrance cleats in place in the spring as long as the weather remains cold and the colony population is not so great that the cleats must be removed. Chilled brood can occur in colonies with large populations as well as those with small populations, though it is more likely to affect the latter. Take care not to divide colonies or to make new increase (new colonies) too early in the spring.

### Mice

In the fall months throughout the northern United States and Canada it is common for mice to move from their field nests into buildings and other areas where they can build better-protected nests for winter. Mice often nest in stored combs and in hives containing bees. It is an interesting fact that mice can successfully build a nest within a honey bee colony with a strong population and yet survive the winter without difficulty and without being stung by the bees. However, the mice are protected by a thick layer of nesting material and no doubt move in and out of the colony entrance at a time when the bees are inactive. Try to eliminate mice from the vicinity of the apiary as much as is possible. Mowing the grass around colonies has been suggested as one way to reduce mouse damage. Apparently, mice prefer to live where there is overgrowth and do not care to cross open, mowed grass for fear of being exposed and caught by a predator. (For more on mice, see Chapter 7, "Wintering Honey Bees.")

### Bears

In mountainous and heavily wooded areas of the United States and Canada, bears are common and they will sometimes attack bee hives. However, not all bears present problems for beekeepers.

Unfortunately, there is no perfect protection against damage by bears. Electric fences have been devised to keep bears out of apiaries, but their cost is too high for most beekeepers. Except under special circumstances and for

A "bear-resistant" cage was built around these colonies being used for blueberry pollination in Florida. However, it didn't work: the bears tore apart the cage and enjoyed the honey!

short-term use, the return a beekeeper can expect for investing in a bear fence is not sufficient to warrant its construction. Bears are wary animals, and are less inclined to attack bee hives in the vicinity of a house or barn; however, this is not always an effective measure for keeping bears out of an apiary.

In some states, conservation departments trap nuisance bears in large, humane-style traps and move them to areas where they presumably will not pose a problem. However, bears have been known to walk long distances to reach a good source of food. In a small number of states beekeepers may shoot offending bears, though sometimes a permit is required.

At least four states—Pennsylvania, Vermont, New Hampshire, and Minnesota—compensate beekeepers for losses they incur as a result of bear damage. The reasoning behind these laws is that bears are protected for hunting purposes and that the state should be liable for their depredations. Unfortunately, not all conservation departments share this view, and, where compensation is paid by county governments, you may find differences in attitude and policy from one county to the next.

*Bears have attacked and destroyed a colony in this apiary in Maine. A bear will usually take only one to three hives a night, but will feed for many days until all of the colonies are destroyed.*

People whose colonies have suffered damage from bears report that the bears will pick up and carry these colonies as much as 200 yards from an apiary before dashing them apart on the ground. It is also generally agreed that when a bear begins to work in an apiary, it takes only one to three colonies a night, and continues to do so until the whole apiary is destroyed. While the bears may be stung considerably, this does not seem to deter them. Despite their great liking for brood, there is no doubt that the bears consume honey and also eat some adult bees.

### Skunks

Common skunks, like bears, are primarily meat eaters and live largely on insects and small animals that they are able to catch. Skunks are a serious problem for beekeepers in certain areas of the country. The skunk usually feeds in the evening, scratching on the hive entrance so as to disturb the bees and cause them to fly out or to move to the hive entrance to determine the source of the annoyance. The skunks swat and attempt to kill the bees as they crawl through the entrance hole of their hive and then eat them.

Skunks have been dissected, and it has been found that their tongues, mouths, throats, and stomachs all had bee stings, but apparently their gustatory liking for the insect was so great that this did not deter them. People who have observed skunks feeding have noted that they roll, twist, and turn on the ground in front of the hive as they are stung by other bees coming from the hive. Evidence that skunks have been feeding on colonies of honey bees can be seen by observing the entrance and the grass immediately in front of it. The entrance of the colony is usually covered with mud, and the grass and sod are torn up in front of the bee hive.

It is difficult to control skunk feeding, but when nothing is done, weak colonies may be killed. The skunk's feeding irritates the bees and may keep a colony in a constant state of alarm, under which circumstances it is difficult to work in an apiary because of constant attacks by guard bees. Beekeepers report receiving many more stings in an apiary where skunks are feeding because the bees are always on the alert. Not too many years ago beekeepers routinely poisoned predatory skunks, but this practice is now illegal in some areas. Consult your local county extension agent or agricultural advisor on how best to deal with the problem. Moving colonies, fencing an apiary, or elevating colonies may prevent skunk damage, but these are costly and not very practical measures. Skunks should not be trapped unless you are willing to tolerate the odor of trapped skunk for many weeks thereafter.

### Squirrels

Red squirrels can be a serious menace to bee equipment stored in buildings, especially outbuildings that are not inspected very frequently. The squirrels find a building a dry place in which to nest, and during the winter months they can chew and destroy many combs, presumably to obtain honey and pollen for food. Most beekeepers leave poison wheat or bait in their buildings to kill any rats or mice; however, squirrels usually do not eat such bait. Storage buildings should have cement floors and be carefully screened to prevent entry by squirrels and other rodents. Seek professional advice from an agricultural agent or advisor to determine what means you can legally use to control these pests. Squirrels can sometimes be trapped in humane traps using nuts as bait.

### Wax moths

Wax moths, or wax worms (*Galleria mellonella*), originated in Asia, but are now widespread around the world. The adult females fly into bee hives at

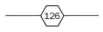

dusk and deposit their eggs. The larvae burrow deep into the comb and can often complete their development without being detected by the bees. In colonies that are weak, or dead, the wax moth larvae will soon reduce the comb to frass (fecal matter) and tangled webbing.

The best protection against wax moths is to have strong colonies that can remove their larvae as soon as they appear. Some fumigants for wax moths are available, but keeping supers of combs on colonies is still the best protection.

## PESTICIDES

Several insecticides have presented a serious problem for beekeepers for over a century. However, since the formation of the federal Environmental Protection Agency in 1970, and the passage of laws requiring that pesticides toxic to honey bees carry warning labels, there have been fewer problems. Beekeepers in intense agricultural areas, such as parts of Texas, Arizona, California, and Washington, still complain about some insecticides such as Penncap-M and Sevin. However, many fewer complaints are heard today from all parts of the country than were received just a few years ago.

Warning labels on insecticide packages make it clear that users are responsible for any damage they may cause. Most labels on pesticides toxic to honey bees state that the material should not be applied or allowed to drift onto blooming crops or weeds.

Perhaps more important is the fact that fruit and vegetable growers today are more aware than ever that honey bees are essential for pollination and that the bees must be protected. Over a million colonies of bees are moved each year to pollinate crops in almost every state.

Most of the pesticides that are harmful to honey bees, kill the bees slowly over a period of one or more days. As a result, when a pesticide kill occurs you may see one to several thousand bees in a pile, up to 3 feet in front of a hive. Under normal circumstances, you would expect to find fewer than 15 to 20 fresh bees dead in front of a colony on a typical morning when pesticides are not a problem. The enforcers of the label laws are usually the state departments of conservation or agriculture, who should be notified if a pesticide loss is seen or suspected. It is usually possible to detect the pesticide in the dead bees if a sample of several hundred bees is taken and frozen on the same day the kill occurs.

## DISEASE DIAGNOSIS

As was stated earlier, many state departments of agriculture are less helpful in bee disease control today because of changing priorities in the way tax monies are spent. For most of this century, states and Canadian provinces have felt that the maintenance of a healthy beekeeping industry was in everyone's best interest. Even though at present there is a greater demand for bees for pollination then ever before, there is less interest in honey bee disease control.

In recent years, several states and Canadian provinces have published bulletins and brochures on bee disease identification and control. Some of these publications contain color plates illustrating the disease symptoms and sometimes the organism that causes the problem. It is suggested that bee-keepers obtain some of these bulletins and start building up a small library on bee disease identification and control. Beekeepers must face the fact that they are often on their own in controlling pests, predators, and diseases of honey bees. However, aid in diagnosing bee diseases is available from one federal laboratory. (See "The Federal Laboratories" in Chapter 14.)

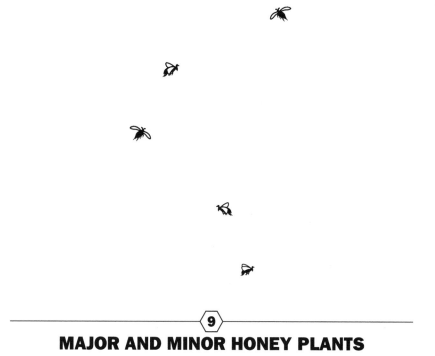

---
⬡ 9 ⬡
---

# MAJOR AND MINOR HONEY PLANTS

ONEY BEES FEED EXCLUSIVELY ON NECTAR AND pollen. Nectar is made into honey and is their source of carbohydrates. This is discussed more fully in Chapter 5. Pollen provides the protein and the small amount of fat that bees need to survive. In this chapter we are concerned primarily with the more important nectar sources.

Many plants produce nectar from glands (nectaries) located in their flowers. Nectar is a reward given to the bees by plants for carrying pollen, the male germ cells, from one flower to another. There are more than 2,000 plants in the United States that produce nectar, pollen, or nectar and pollen. However, only a small number of these, about 35, produce enough nectar, or are sufficiently abundant that bees, and hence beekeepers, rely on them for a crop. This is not to downplay the significance of the minor honey plants, though, for they are important for the day-to-day existence of many colonies.

It is not profitable to plant plants for honey production. Beekeepers are content either to adjust their colony numbers to the food sources available or to move their colonies to areas where honey plants abound. About half of the honey produced in the United States comes from weed plants and the rest from cultivated crops. White Dutch clover, the most important honey plant in the country, occurs as a weed in lawns and is an important pasture and hay plant.

Weather has a profound effect on nectar secretion; too much or too little water, and cool or warm temperature, all influence nectar secretion. Wind may cause nectar to dry to the extent that bees cannot collect it. Soil type is important, too. The various clovers, for example, secrete the greatest quantity of nectar when growing on sweet (non-acid), well-drained soil. Thus, just because a plant is present in an area does not mean that honey will be produced from it.

The honey crop in the United States varies from about 160 to 250 million pounds per year. California is usually the leading state, producing anywhere from10 to 20 million pounds a year. This is a great, but normal

Stigma — Style — Nectar — Anther — Ovary

*An orange blossom with some of the anthers removed. Note the glistening nectar and flower's ovary that will develop into an orange.*

variation. Even in a good year the percentages of honey produced from different plants will rarely be the same as in previous years.

## THE MOST IMPORTANT HONEY PLANTS

The plants on this list are those that, in a normal year, are responsible for the production of half a million or more pounds of honey in North America; some, of course, produce much more. I have placed these plants into three groups, according to their importance.

### *The clovers and alfalfa*

*The following represent the most important North American honey plants. They are responsible for about 55 percent of the total honey production; alfalfa is responsible for 10 to 15 percent of the total.*

> clovers
>> *white clover (white Dutch clover)*
>> *white sweet clover*
>> *alsike clover*
>> *yellow sweet clover*
>> *a mixture of several other clovers*
> alfalfa

### *The oilseed plants*

*The following, as a group, have become increasingly important as North Americans have started to consume more seed oils. This group is probably responsible for 10 percent of the total honey production. This figure may increase slightly as the public demands certain features (lower cholesterol, etc.) in the edible oils it consumes.*

> rapeseed and canola *(canola is a selected variety of rapeseed)*
> safflower
> soybeans
> sunflower
> other oilseed plants

### *Miscellaneous (500,000 to 6 million pounds each)*

*The following plants are responsible for about 35 percent of the total honey crop.*

> aster
> basswood *(becoming more common in the East as natural reforestation occurs)*

In this picture we see a typical apiary in a Georgia flatwoods that is being used for package bee production.

Brazilian pepper tree *(recent Florida freezes have greatly reduced production)*

buckwheat, wild western *(primarily in California; not the same as the eastern buckwheat species)*

catclaw acacia

cotton

fireweed

gallberry *(one of the more important plants in this group)*

goldenrod *(was once more important)*

locust *(mostly black locust)*

mangrove *(becoming less common as seashore areas are developed)*

mesquite

milkweed

orange blossom *(citrus)*

palmetto

purple loosestrife

raspberry and blackberry

sages *(several species, one of the more important plants in this group)*

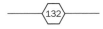

salt cedar

sourwood *(not a consistent yielder, but a high-priced honey)*

Spanish needle

sumac

tallow tree *(Chinese tallow)*

thistle *(several species)*

titi *(the most important plant in this group, producing an estimated
6 million pounds annually)*

tupelo *(traditionally the most expensive honey in the United States, but
produced in quantity only in a small area of west Florida)*

tulip tree

vetch *(several species)*

yellow star thistle

## The "has beens"

*The following plants have become "has beens" because of changes in
American agriculture. For example, in about 1900 the beekeeper with the
greatest number of colonies in the country lived in Ithaca, New York; he had
4,000 colonies and produced great quantities of buckwheat honey. At the
time, the area around Ithaca was heavily farmed, only 20 percent of the land
was wooded, and buckwheat was a common grain on almost every farm.
Today, however, the area has been virtually abandoned insofar as agriculture is
concerned and 50 percent of the land is wooded.*

*Wild thyme was once important in the East too, but that was 40 or more
years ago when the Catskill Mountains area of New York State was heavily
involved in dairying and cows were pastured; the cows ate almost all of the
plants in a pasture except the thyme, which was apparently not tasty to them;
as a result, the thyme plants flourished. Today, beekeepers keep only five to
ten colonies in wild thyme apiaries that once supported sixty or more.*

buckwheat, eastern cultivated varieties *(will probably never be important again as a honey plant; there is little research on buckwheat ,
and it is of little interest to plant breeders, who do not see a market
for it)*

wild thyme *(widespread in the East, but cannot stand competition from
other plants)*

heartsease

## NOTES ON SOME IMPORTANT SPRING BUILD-UP PLANTS

Beekeepers are very much aware that, in some years, a large quantity of honey is made from nectar secreted by a host of early spring plants including apple, willow, dandelion, yellow rocket, locust, and others. Which plants are important to your bees depends on where you live. However, honey flows from these plants are highly weather-dependent, and the quantity of honey produced from them varies greatly from year to year. Yet, these secondary honey plants are still important because the surpluses they produce are usually needed to grow the bees that will in turn harvest the primary honey flows to follow.

## HONEYDEW HONEY

Honeydew honey is made from a nectar or sweet substance produced by something other than nectaries in flowers. However, there are plant glands, not associated with flowers, that are found on stems and leaves and secrete a nectar, or at least a nectar-like substance, that bees can make into honey. The cotton plant, for example, often has a number of extra floral nectaries on its stems. These are in addition to its regular floral nectaries.

Botanists have proposed many theories as to why plants may have evolved extra floral nectaries. If one accepts the point of view that most plant and animal structures have a purpose, then the most obvious explanation is that extra floral nectars may serve to attract ants, wasps, and honey bees, all stinging insects that might serve to scare or even sting animals that might otherwise feed on the plant's foliage. In this way the stinging insects may serve the same function as physical structures like thorns, to discourage browsing. This simple explanation is not accepted by everyone, but it is one to which I subscribe. Because these extra floral nectaries secrete a substance that is the same, or at least little different from that produced in floral nectaries, many people feel that the honey produced from it should not be called "honeydew honey." Indeed, this is not an unreasonable position, as honey from these nectar sources is often as good as the best floral honeys.

The substance most accurately referred to as *honeydew* is collected by honey bees from secretions produced by insects such as aphids, leafhoppers, and scales. These insects feed on plant saps and obtain both proteins and carbohydrates from them. Apparently, they obtain more sugar than they need, and this sugar is then secreted as waste material onto the plant's leaves or needles. In some cases there may be so much honeydew that it drips off the leaves and onto the ground. Honeydew may attract a wide variety of insects. Honey made by bees from honeydew is usually high in protein, dark in color, and strong in flavor. Beekeepers usually try to use honeydew honey as bee food, though some of it may be harvested and find its way into the bakery trade.

Honeydew honey is highly regarded by many people in Germany, Poland, Switzerland, and certain other northern European countries, where it is often produced in quantity. The reason for great quantities of honeydew being produced in these countries is that the planted forests may consist of only one, two, or three tree species. Such concentrations of a single plant species often attract harmful pests, which are usually not so abundant in mixed forests such as we have in much of the United States and southern Canada. In Europe, honeydew honey is called "forest honey." Its dark, strong flavor is well known and well liked by many people, who may seek it out in the market. As a result, beekeepers often move their colonies into forested areas for the honeydew honey flow. Colonies of bees have been known to perish during long honeydew flows, as little or no pollen is produced in these areas and the bees cannot grow enough young bees to replace those that die. Since the hard work of foraging shortens the life of the field bees, replacement bees are needed. A lack of young bees can often be a serious problem for beekeepers who rely on honeydew flows.

## GOVERNMENT ERADICATION AND CONTROL PROJECTS

A small number of the major and minor honey plants in the United States and Canada are considered noxious weeds by persons other than beekeepers. Beekeepers consider a lawn full of flowering dandelions or white Dutch clover as a beautiful sight and fail to understand why anyone would want to eliminate these colorful flowers.

However, beyond these two rather benign plants, there are other plants that are sufficiently objectionable under some circumstances that the federal government, and some state governments, are trying to eliminate them, or at least reduce their numbers. Some of the plants on the government's "bad" list include purple loosestrife, cajeput (melaleuca), mesquite, Brazilian pepper tree, salt cedar, two species of knapweed, and three

species of thistles. The list of plants prepared under the 1974 Federal Noxious Weed Act no doubt includes many more minor nectar and pollen plants as well.

## SCALE HIVES

Beekeepers and experimentalists have often kept colonies of honey bees on scales and measured daily or weekly weight gains and losses. Since a colony may gain 10 or more pounds on a single day during a good nectar flow, it is not difficult to measure a colony's activity using a scale hive. (For more information, refer to "Weighing colonies" in Chapter 7.)

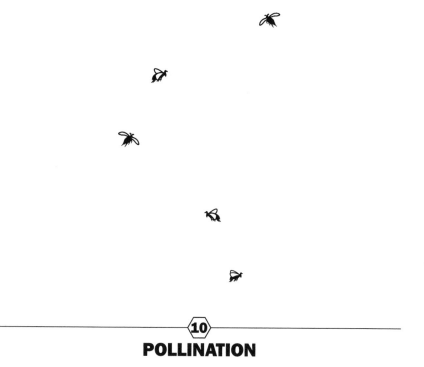

# 10

# POLLINATION

POLLINATION IS THE MOVEMENT OF POLLEN FROM the male to the female parts of plants. Plants vary greatly. In some, the male and female parts are located within the same flower, while in others separate male and female flowers are on the same plant. There are even some plants that are entirely male and female, but as beekeepers we are usually little concerned with this last group, since their pollen is normally carried by the wind from one plant to another. However, these wind-pollinated plants often produce great quantities of pollen, which bees sometimes collect and use as food. Corn is an example of one wind-pollinated plant that may produce over 400 pounds of pollen per acre. Since it is airborne, corn pollen is usually too dry for bees to collect, but if it is wetted by a light rain or a heavy dew, the bees will collect it in quantity.

## OUR CHANGING AGRICULTURE

Food is cheaper in the United States than in any other country because of our intense, specialized agricultural system, of which honey bees are very much a part. One-third of the colonies of bees in the United States, over 1 million colonies, are rented for crop pollination each year. Most of these colonies are used on two, and sometimes even three crops. Pollination is primarily a springtime business, since the fruits, nuts, and berries on the pollinated crops must have time to mature. Only a small number of colonies are used for greenhouse pollination in winter.

Bees have been trucked from Texas to California and from Florida to Maine for the purposes of pollination. The crops for which the greatest number of colonies are used are listed below:

| Crop | Number of colonies |
|---|---|
| almonds | 650,000 |
| apples | 250,000 |
| melons | 250,000 |
| alfalfa seed | 220,000 |
| plums/prunes | 145,000 |
| avocados | 100,000 |
| blueberries | 75,000 |
| cherries | 70,000 |
| vegetable seeds | 50,000 |
| pears | 50,000 |
| cucumbers | 40,000 |
| sunflowers | 40,000 |
| cranberries | 30,000 |
| kiwi fruit | 15,000 |
| others | 50,000 |

**Note:** *These data are taken from the following paper: W. S. Robinson, R. Nowogrodzki, and R. A. Morse. "The value of honey bees as pollinators of U. S. crops." American Bee Journal 129: 411–23, 477–87. 1989.*

*The small, inadequately pollinated apple on the left has only one seed. Apples may have as many as ten seeds but an apple with seven or eight, as is illustrated on the right, will usually be of normal size and shape.*

These figures demonstrate the tremendous revolution that has taken place in U.S. agriculture in this century. Bees were not rented for pollination prior to 1909, when the first record was made of a few colonies being rented for apple pollination in New Jersey. Yet today, the number of colonies being used for pollination is increasing rapidly. For example, the number used for lowbush blueberry pollination in Maine has increased by about 1,000 colonies each year during the past several years, with 35,000 colonies transported into that state, mostly from Florida, for that purpose in 1993.

We have no figures concerning the value of honey bees to home gardens and commercial farms. Many colonies are kept adjacent to such areas by both commercial beekeepers and hobbyists, whose chief concern is honey production and who receive no compensation for their bees' work other than the use of an apiary site. However, these bees make a real contribution to both home gardens and commercial farms. Their true dollar value is probably even greater than that earned by rented colonies. Beekeepers also make an unknown contribution to the pollination of wild fruits, nuts, and seeds used by wildlife.

Honey bees are not the only insects that are important as pollinators in modern agriculture, but they are certainly the chief contributors. They are also easily moved and manipulated. Colonies of honey bees are ready for work at any time of the year. In an emergency, colonies may be carried north and south, east and west, with little difficulty.

*This worker honey bee is gathering nectar from an apple blossom. Apple blossoms are not sufficiently numerous, or bee colonies strong enough in the spring, to make apple blossom honey in sufficient quantity that it may be harvested.*

## THE PROPER SIZE COLONY FOR POLLINATION

A colony of honey bees used for pollination must have a population large enough to do an adequate job. However, it must be of a size small enough so that it can be easily moved. Also, the colony must not be congested or it will swarm. Not only does swarming deplete a population, but for many days before a colony swarms its field force gorges on honey and is largely inactive.

By tradition, a colony used for pollination usually occupies two 8- or 10-frame Langstroth supers. However, for crops pollinated early in the season the colony may be contained in only one super, not having had the time to build up a stronger population. Colonies used for apple pollination, for example, will usually occupy two supers and contain about 20,000 to 30,000 worker bees and a queen.

## PREPARING COLONIES FOR POLLINATION

Colonies used for pollination should be inspected within a week or two of being moved. The beekeeper needs to make certain the colony is queen right (i.e. has a laying queen), has sufficient food in the event of a dearth, and is free, or relatively free, of any major disease. In the case of mites, for example, one never expects to rid a colony of all such pests.

In most pollination situations, rented colonies of bees have brood in six frames, which is used as a measure of their population and strength. It is important to note that this does not mean six frames full of brood. Since a honey bee colony brood nest is the shape of a ball, or football, the two outer frames will contain only a small amount of brood, while the two center frames may be 70 to 80 percent full. It is more difficult to measure the size of a brood nest if it stretches across two supers, but even in this situation the brood nest will retain its ball-like shape.

## THE TEMPORARY APIARY SITE

Selecting a site for bees in a field to be pollinated is little, if any, different from selecting a permanent site for colonies. One seeks the same qualities: a maximum of sunlight, a slope to the east or south, proximity to a clean source of water, and a good access road.

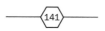

*These four colonies on a pallet in an orange grove in Florida have been moved on and off of a truck with a forklift thus saving labor.*

## USING PACKAGE BEES FOR POLLINATION

Packages of bees are not satisfactory for pollination because there are too few bees in a package, and they will not have brood for several days after they are installed. Bees rearing brood need pollen and are stimulated to go foraging in the field to find it. A 3-pound package of bees contains about 12,000 bees. Nearly half of these individuals will die in the first three weeks after the package is installed and before replacement bees will emerge from the cells to take up hive chores.

## SUBSOCIAL AND SOLITARY BEES AS POLLINATORS

Bumble bees and a great number of solitary ground- and twig-nesting bees are important pollinators in most parts of the country. Bumble bee colonies are sometimes sold for greenhouse pollination. One species of leaf-cutter bee is widely used in some western states for alfalfa pollination. However, all of these bees require careful management and a thorough knowledge of their biology to be used successfully. Because this is true, honey bees are usually the bees of choice when pollinators are needed.

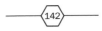

## METHODS OF MOVING BEES

Colonies of honey bees used for pollination are usually moved in from another site. Most are transported at night, since all of the bees are in their hives at that time. The hives may be screened and confined individually or they may be loaded onto a truck and the whole load covered with a screen. More information on moving bees can be found under "Migratory bee-keeping" in Chapter 11.

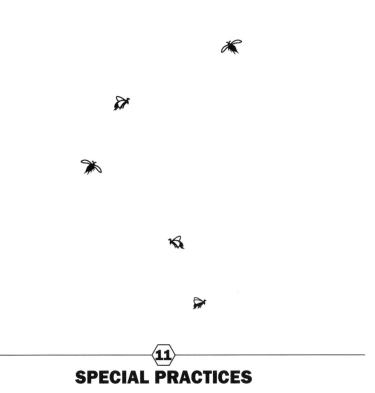

# 11

# SPECIAL PRACTICES

PRODUCING HONEY IS THE REASON MOST PEOPLE FIRST become interested in beekeeping. There are, however, a number of related activities for both hobbyists and commercial beekeepers. Certain of these are dependent upon location and local need. Hundreds of books and papers have been written about some of the subjects discussed below. A valuable source of information, if you care to pursue a particular subject further, is your county's agricultural extension agents and the apiculturists at the state colleges.

## BEESWAX: PRODUCTION AND USES

For every 100 pounds of honey produced, you will usually harvest one to

two pounds of beeswax from the cappings that are cut from the combs of ripe honey. Cappings wax is of high quality. Some beeswax is also rendered from old and broken combs, but this is usually darker in color than cappings wax and more heavily stained with propolis. Dark wax is of less value. In some years as much as 5 percent of a beekeeper's income may come from the beeswax that is produced.

Worker honey bees have four pairs of wax glands on the undersides of their abdomens. Wax is produced only as it is needed to build new comb or to cap cells filled with honey. Bees usually use old wax to cap the cells of developing pupae.

Beeswax is a complex substance with over 300 separate components, not one of which is present to the extent of more than about 8 percent. When beeswax is secreted by honey bees it is a clear liquid that solidifies and turns white when it is exposed to the air. The beeswax collected from a hive is yellow because it is stained by pollen and propolis. The delicate, pleasing odor from a burning beeswax candle is largely the odor of burning propolis.

The chief use of beeswax today is to make comb foundation, which in turn is used by bees to make new combs. The second largest use is the manufacture of beeswax candles. Many beekeepers make candles for their own use or to sell. Candles may be rolled from sheets of wax or they may be dipped or molded. Molded candles are the easiest to make, as molds are readily available. A note of caution, though: beeswax burns, and you need to exercise considerable care when melting and pouring hot, molten wax. Also, you should always avoid an open flame when melting beeswax as it may easily catch fire.

Beeswax was mankind's first plastic and served in a variety of roles. For example, it was used in writing tablets, in batik designs on fabric, in grafting wax, in encaustic painting, and to wax threads. One of its more important uses historically was in the "lost wax" process of sculpting. When bronze, gold, or iron statues were made, the first step was to sculpt the model in beeswax. This wax figure was then covered with wet clay and baked. The wax was "lost" from the mold as it was heated and then the clay mold was used for the final metal casting. This process is still used in some parts of the world today.

*Here are two queen cells on wooden cell bases. A queen has emerged from the cell on the right.*

## QUEEN REARING

A fertilized egg laid by a queen honey bee develops into either a worker or another queen, depending upon the food it receives during its larval stage. When this fact was first discovered in the 1800s, beekeepers attempted to rear queens. For many years the only technique they used was to divide a colony and to allow the bees in the queenless half to rear a new queen, a method still used today in parts of the world where queens are not readily available.

Practical methods of rearing queens were discovered in 1883, when Henry Alley of Massachusetts found that he could introduce pieces of comb cut into strips, with eggs in alternating cells, which would be accepted and enlarged by colonies of queenless bees to produce queen cells. A few years later, G. M. Doolittle discovered a method of making artificial queen cups and of *grafting* (moving) young worker larvae into these. By the late 1800s, the business of queen rearing had become well developed, and large numbers of queen bees were being shipped by mail. The basic techniques of rearing queens developed back then are still being widely used today.

People who rear queens are well aware of the fact that better queens are produced when there is an abundant supply of both pollen and nectar. While queen larvae are reared largely on a diet of royal jelly, a glandular secretion from worker bees, workers cannot produce this secretion without an abundance of food. Studies have shown that queens produced from well-fed larvae are larger and have more ovarioles per ovary. It is presumed that queens with more ovarioles produce more eggs. Queen breeders usually keep sugar syrup feeders in queen rearing colonies as a safeguard. But, even more importantly, breeders select queen rearing areas because they have an abundant supply of both pollen- and nectar-producing plants during the queen rearing season, which runs from February through May and, to a lesser extent, in June, July, and August.

Rearing queens involves transferring about 24-hour-old worker larvae from their cells into slightly larger, artificially made queen cups (a procedure known as grafting). The queen cups are then placed in colonies of queenless bees, which usually accept and feed the larvae lavishly. After 24 to 48 hours in the so-called *starter colonies*, the newly grafted larvae are transferred into what are called *finishing colonies*. While starter colonies have no free flight, finishing colonies are queenless, but the bees are allowed to fly. The larvae in the queen cells continue to be fed by workers in the finishing colonies, and the cells are capped with beeswax on the fifth day of large life. One day before the pupae are due to emerge from their cells, (which is 15 days after the egg has been laid by the queen), the finished queen cells are removed from the colonies in which they have been nurtured and they are placed individually in *mating nuclei*. Mating nuclei are boxes that usually contain small pieces of comb, a limited quantity of honey and pollen, and 500 to 1,000 or more bees. The virgin queens that emerge in these nuclei are fed and cared for by the workers in them. It is from these small mating nuclei that the virgin queens take flight and subsequently mate. When the queen rearer finds that the newly mated queens are laying eggs, the queens are placed in queen cages together with five or six worker bees and sold.

Queen rearing requires some special equipment. Because so few people do this commercially, the equipment is not generally available, and queen breeders usually build their own special frames, cell bars, and queen-mating nucleus boxes. Wax and plastic cups, into which young lar-

*This rack in a 2-inch-deep bottomboard is used to deter comb building below the brood nest. Deeper bottomboards are used in comb honey production for better ventilation.*

vae are grafted, are available from the commercial bee supply companies, but many beekeepers make their own using pure beeswax. The same companies also make the queen cages in which queens are mailed; however, the equipment used between grafting and mailing the mated queen is largely a product of the queen breeder's workshop.

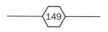

*Old-fashioned rectangular comb honey sections such as these into which foundation is being placed were once very popular in the United States. However, it is more expensive to produce comb honey than it is liquid honey, so it has become less popular today.*

Queen rearing requires considerable attention to detail, especially insofar as removing the ripe queen cells from the colony is concerned, so that the emerging virgin queens do not kill one another. However, many beekeepers with only a few colonies routinely grow their own queens. Successful commercial queen rearing requires the development of a market, though the existing bee journals provide sufficient advertising media. This market could be expanded in the North.

## COMB HONEY PRODUCTION

At the turn of the century, almost all of the honey produced in the United States was sold as comb honey (honey in the comb). While the favorite size of comb honey section contained 13 to 14 ounces of honey in square or rectangular wooden boxes, comb honey was also made in 2-pound sections and, rarely, in ¼- and ½-pound sections. Beekeepers produced comb honey because liquid honey was frequently adulterated with cheaper sugars. The first of the Pure Food and Drug Laws was not passed by the United States Congress until 1906, and until then beekeepers had no way of protecting themselves against this adulteration. However, consumers understood that honey sold in the comb was pure.

Following the passage of the Pure Food and Drug Laws, the market for liquid honey increased slowly. During World War I there was a greater demand for honey as the sugar supply in the United States was reduced due to the war's effect on commercial shipping. Since it is cheaper and easier to produce liquid rather than comb honey, many beekeepers began to do so at that time. Their efforts intensified for the same reasons during World War II. As a result, almost no one in the United States today makes a full-time living producing comb honey; however, comb honey production is a favorite pastime for many amateur beekeepers. When there is a good local retail market, comb honey production can also be a profitable sideline. The production of comb honey, generally speaking, costs much more per pound than does the production of liquid honey, but the sale price is also much greater.

As one examines the beekeeping industry, it is difficult to say whether the production of queens or the production of comb honey represents the more difficult aspect of the art. Certainly both queen rearing and comb honey production require considerable attention to detail. Comb honey producers must understand the biology of the colony and must be in a position to make close examinations of the brood nest during the active honey flow when the sections are being filled.

Successful comb honey producers reduce the brood nest to one deep super one to two days after the start of a major honey flow, and again at the time when the comb honey supers are added to the colony. Young queens are much less inclined to swarm than old queens and, since crowding encourages swarming, you must try to have young queens in your colonies at the start of the honey flow. Frames containing capped brood are placed in the single brood-nest super so that the bees in them will emerge as soon as possible and add to the overall population of the colony. This also provides a place for the queen to lay eggs in an otherwise crowded hive. Even with as many precautions as the beekeeper can take, it is necessary to examine each comb in the brood nest at intervals of seven to eight days during the honey flow. Any queen cells produced by the bees must be removed. While removing cells does not guarantee that a swarm will not depart from the hive, it usually prevents swarming.

During the honey flow the supers must be rotated and those with filled sections removed as soon as the bees have capped them. Since the final package is sold to the consumer in the wood or plastic that surrounds it in the hive, it is extremely important that it be kept clean and that the

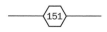

amount of travel stain on the comb be kept at a minimum.

Comb honey producers have several problems not encountered by the producers of liquid honey. In years past it was recommended that comb honey sections be fumigated before they were marketed; today there is no product that is approved for comb honey fumigation. The only recourse is for the beekeeper to place comb honey sections in a freezer for 24 hours or more to kill any wax moth eggs or larvae that may be present.

Premature granulation of honey in the comb can also be a serious problem. For this reason, comb honey is usually moved to the market and sold as rapidly as possible. Some honeys granulate more rapidly than others, and you should be aware of the major honey-producing plants in your area. Comb honey is a delicate product, and it is not advisable to ship it by routine shipping methods.

Still, there are few things in beekeeping today that can give greater satisfaction than the production of a super of fine comb honey. Not only is there a good demand for comb honey, but it makes an unusual gift. Since honey in the comb is unprocessed, it retains its delicate flavor and is an unusual, natural product.

Like the processes used to rear queens, those for producing comb honey were developed in the late 1800s. Several books have been written on the subject of comb honey production (see "Books" in Chapter 14). Several states have issued bulletins on the subject, and articles on comb honey production appear frequently in the bee journals.

### Round sections

In 1954, 4-inch-diameter plastic round sections for comb honey were invented. They have several virtues. They contain 7 to 8 ounces of honey versus 12 to 14 ounces in square or rectangular sections, but they usually sell for about the same price. The section supers and their furniture are easier to assemble and clean. Honey bees do a better job of filling the round sections, as they are not accustomed to working in square corners such as occur in wooden sections. For the best results, the same intensive management scheme, which involves the crowding of the colonies, is needed.

### Chunk and cut comb honey production

Cut comb honey is composed of comb chunks, usually containing between 2 and 16 ounces of honey each. These pieces of comb are cut from much larger combs, produced in standard half-depth frames that measure about 4" x 17". The individual pieces of comb are cut with a hot knife, and the honey from the cut cells is allowed to drain for up to 24 hours before the individual pieces are wrapped in cellophane or plastic. The wrapped pieces of cut comb are normally protected by cardboard for shipping. Cut comb honey has most of the advantages of comb honey, especially in flavor and appearance, but the production techniques are much easier.

Chunk honey is a piece or pieces of cut comb honey placed in a jar and surrounded by liquid honey. Chunk honey packs have been favorites in the southern states for decades. However, most of the honeys produced in the southern states are much slower to granulate than those produced in the northern states and Canada. Thus, a chunk honey pack would have a shelf life of four to six months in the South, while in the North a similar pack might have a shelf life of only a few weeks. A granulated chunk honey pack has little appeal to the average purchaser.

Producers of combs of honey to be cut into smaller pieces usually follow the same management techniques used by comb honey producers; however, it is not necessary to pay quite so much attention to detail. The fact that there are no dividers or fences between the combs, as there are in comb honey supers, makes the chunk honey supers less crowded, and swarming is not as much of a problem. Chunk-honey producers do not need to crowd their colonies to force the bees to fill every section. Pieces of comb not perfectly filled may be trimmed or not used at all without too much monetary loss. When you produce comb honey, however, you cannot afford to discard too many sections, just because of the extra cost of the plastic or wood and the labor involved in preparing the supers.

It is possible to produce a few frames of chunk honey by placing the frames in the center of an ordinary extracting honey super. If you plan to do this, the super should have only light-colored combs on either side of the frames in which chunk honey is to be produced; otherwise, the chunk-honey frames will become travel-stained and will not have a good appearance. When a light-colored comb is placed next to an old, dark comb, it can be observed that bees just walking from one comb to another will carry enough residue on their feet to stain the new comb. Removing the newly filled comb, in the case of the production of both comb honey and chunk honey, is advisable for the same reason.

## SHOWING HONEY

Honey shows are often popular at agricultural fairs and at many beekeepers meetings. Not only is a honey show at a fair an excellent method of advertising honey, but often sales from the show booths can be profitable. Also, honey shows offer an opportunity for beekeepers to improve their methods of packing and preparing for market through observation of what others are doing.

Where possible, it is advisable to require the judge to use a grading card and to assign points in each category. It is only by doing so that the beekeeper can learn where errors were made and where emphasis should be placed to improve the quality of future entries. It is also helpful for both the participants and the judge if the rules for the show are printed and available to everyone well before the show. Some of the items that should be predetermined are the size and type of jar and cap, the number of jars for each entry (three is the usual number), when the entries are due, and how moisture content is to be judged.

## MIGRATORY BEEKEEPING

Migratory beekeeping has been practiced for several thousand years. The Egyptians apparently moved their bees on barges on the Nile River when their civilization was at its peak. It has been shown that colonies of honey bees can be transported over long or short distances without harm to the bees, brood, or stored food. It is necessary to move colonies more than two or three miles; otherwise the field bees will fly back (drift) to their original location.

The rapidity with which field bees adapt to new foraging conditions is remarkable. While many of the bees in a colony tend to be quite angry and very prone to sting for several hours immediately after the colony is moved to a new location, many of the worker bees will start to forage immediately. Observations by several people indicate that foraging bees can return to newly moved hives with pollen loads within 15 minutes after being moved and released in a new location.

The danger in moving a colony to a new location is not chilling the brood, but overheating the colony. When colonies are being moved from one location to another, a cluster will form in each hive if there is danger of chilling the brood. Within the cluster heat is generated, and in this way

*Here is a colony with a top screen that is properly stapled for moving.*

the brood is protected. However, bees cannot guard against overheating as easily. If the bees are unable to move large volumes of air through the colony it may overheat, the excess heat being produced by the bees themselves in their unsuccessful attempt to cool the hive. In hives that overheat, the combs may melt and the bees and brood die. For this reason it is safest to move colonies during cool weather and/or at night.

The safest way to move a colony of bees is to smoke it gently and to place it with an open entrance on a truck, cover it with screening, and move it to the new location. It is an interesting fact that the vibration of a truck bed will usually calm the bees and inhibit most flight. Thus, there is not much danger of too many bees being lost from the colony while it is being moved. A major problem with open-entrance moving in warm weather is that large numbers of bees may come out and cluster on the outside of the hive, making it difficult to remove the hive from the truck bed. Smoking the bees on the outside of the hive will cause them to move back inside. Beekeepers who move their colonies open-entrance usually cover the entire truck with a large plastic or wire screen to prevent the bees from escaping from the truck.

*Hive lifters, as shown here, make it easier to move a colony a long or short distance.*

While open-entrance moving is favored by many large-scale beekeepers, the more conventional method is to use a top screen and some type of entrance screen. The top screen is usually made in the shape of a super and has a rim about two inches deep. This rim is covered with some type of wire screening; eight-mesh hardware cloth is toughest and works best for this purpose. If the colonies are placed one on top of another, it is necessary to place slats, at least 2 inches square, between the piles of colonies. Several types of entrance screens may be used, including porch screens and the so-called tuck-in screens. Tuck-in screens are much easier to use and require less time. However, the porch screens are more effective in keeping the bees quiet, and presumably aid in giving the colonies better ventilation. Even where large screens are used, though, some beekeepers wet their colonies externally, and even internally, with water from a garden hose during the heat of the day. While wetting the inside of a hive being moved during warm weather may appear to be an extreme act, it is far better than letting the colony die from overheating. Well over 2 million colonies are moved each year for pollination and honey production. Beekeepers report that chilling the brood is not a serious problem but overheating is.

It is often possible to move one or two colonies of bees without stapling or otherwise nailing the supers and bottomboard and cover together. However, hives can break apart in transit, and moving bees in hives that are not secure is not recommended. If bees have used large quantities of propolis, and if the parts of the hive have not been broken apart in recent weeks, often this glue-like material is sufficient to keep the parts together.

Many beekeepers who practice migratory beekeeping use either plastic or steel strapping or hive staples to tie the parts of the hive together. Hive staples are usually larger than ordinary staples, being about 2 inches long, and they do less damage to the wood. It is possible to fasten the parts of the hive together with wooden slats, and this is satisfactory if only a few colonies are being moved; however, wooden slats usually take up too much room when large numbers of colonies are being moved from one location to another. Beekeepers who move many colonies over long distances usually build special bottomboards for their colonies that are not so cumbersome and bulky as the standard bottomboard. Usually these bottomboards take the form of a combination bottomboard cover and may be easily nailed in place while the colonies are being moved. If large numbers of colonies are being moved long distances, it is advisable to limit the size and weight of the units as much as is possible and practical.

When several colonies are being moved at one time, the entrances of the colonies should be opened at dark, but this may not always be practical. If the entrances of a number of colonies are opened at the same time and on a warm day, when bee flight would be encouraged, many bees may fly from their colonies and be lost, drifting to other colonies. It is usually, though not always, the colonies on the end of a row that "pick up" the greatest number of bees under these circumstances. Placing colonies as far apart as is practical and painting the hive bodies different colors are two techniques used to reduce drifting under these and other circumstances.

## OTHER HIVE PRODUCTS

Pollen, royal jelly, propolis, and bee venom are used by bees because of their special properties. *Pollen* is the honey bee's source of protein and also contains a small amount of fat. *Royal jelly* is secreted by glands in the heads of worker bees. It is a rich, proteinaceous food fed to queen larvae, with a small amount being fed to worker larvae, adult queens, and to some extent other worker bees. *Propolis* is the name given the gums and resins that honey bees collect and use to varnish their hive's interior. Propolis contains several antibiotic substances that protect it and the objects it coats against microbes. Propolis basically gives the hive the same protection these same gummy substances give to tree wounds.

*Venom* is injected into enemies by a sting for the express purpose of killing small intruders and driving large ones away from the nest. Honey bee venom is very different from that produced by yellow jackets and other wasps. Wasp venom is often used to paralyze other insects to keep them alive and fresh for food for the wasp young; this is a method of food preservation. Venoms from wasps, because of this interesting use, are often more toxic to humans than honey bee venom,

These four products are collected and sold by beekeepers in many parts of the world for their presumed medical and therapeutic value. There are hundreds, if not thousands, of testimonials concerning their effectiveness. In the United States, the Food and Drug Administration, as well as other government agencies, have allowed the sale of these products provided packagers make no medical or other claims for them. The claims for health benefits come, of course, from other literature and are well known. The value of these hive products is a matter of personal philosophy and lies in the mind of the user.

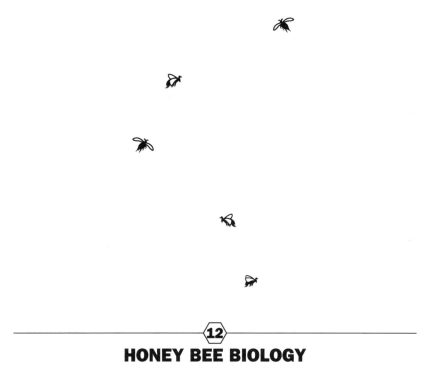

# 12

# HONEY BEE BIOLOGY

AS WE HAVE STATED BEFORE, HONEY BEES ARE NOT domesticated animals. It is possible to keep bees in a hive only because we understand their biology. Beekeeping is the application of our knowledge of bee behavior.

Progress has been made in bee breeding in recent years, but it is a slow process. Certain strains of bees have been selected for their effectiveness as honey gatherers and pollinators, their ability to resist disease, their gentleness, and their adaptation to a wide range of climates. At the present time selecting bees resistant to varroa and tracheal mites is most important. A method of instrumental insemination of queen honey bees has been developed that has been helpful in further exploration. As our knowledge of basic bee biology increases, we should be able to make changes that will benefit both the commercial beekeeper and the hobbyist.

Each member of the honey bee colony is highly specialized and dependent upon all the other members. The queen is an egg-laying machine; additionally, she gives the colony certain chemicals important for the maintenance of social order. The sole function of the drone is to mate. To the worker honey bee fall all other tasks. However, the adaptability of the worker and her ability to change from one task to another with only a few seconds notice are remarkable. Such adaptability is required for the colony to survive during times of stress.

Because the evolutionary pressures on workers, drones, and queens differ, it is only logical that their life histories should vary, too, and that even their development time while in the egg, larval, and pupal stages should not be the same. The following table indicates that the queen develops from an egg into an adult in the shortest time, while the drone takes the longest. The queen is the most important individual in the honey bee colony. From an evolutionary standpoint it makes sense that her development time would be less than that required for the others, since rapid queen replacement can have much to do with the survival of a colony.

Because the sole function of the drone is to mate, and drones are easily reared during the mating season, there has been no evolutionary pressure to speed up their development time.

The number of days required for the development of each type of bee as listed in the following table is reasonably accurate; however, some queens, for example, have been known to develop in only 15½ days. Africanized queens develop even faster, usually in about 15 days. There is some research to suggest that, during the cooler months of the year, worker development may actually be slowed because the bees cannot maintain the brood rearing temperature with ease. However, unlike most insects, whose development time may vary because of fluctuating temperatures, the uniform temperature maintained inside the bee hive means that brood can develop in set periods of time. This fact unquestionably works to the advantage of the honey bee in its competition with other animals.

**HONEY BEE DEVELOPMENT TIME IN DAYS**

|         | Egg | Larva | Pupa | Total Time |
|---------|-----|-------|------|------------|
| Queen   | 3   | 5½    | 7½   | 16         |
| Worker  | 3   | 6     | 12   | 21         |
| Drone   | 3   | 6½    | 14½  | 24         |

## LIFE HISTORY OF THE WORKER

The worker bee is a female. She arises from a fertilized egg. The same egg may produce a worker or a queen depending upon the food received during early larval life. In general, it may be said that a worker honey bee lives for six weeks in the summer and for six months in the winter. (Both of these figures may be a little high.) Like most general statements about animals, it must be understood that this estimated life span involves a great number of variables. In the winter, the worker works less than in the summer, or at least the work done is less wearing on the body. The work done in the summer ages the worker much more rapidly. Old bees can be identified by their physical appearance. They have less body hair than other bees, and their wings may be frayed. Additionally, adult bee diseases may shorten the life of worker bees. Nosema, paralysis, and many lesser maladies play important roles in this regard. Adult bee diseases are especially a problem when colonies are under stress. (For a discussion of bee diseases, see Chapter 8.)

In the active season, a worker honey bee undertakes a long series of duties after her emergence from her cell. These usually follow a set pattern; however, one of the marvels of the hive is the fact that a worker bee may change occupations, sometimes within seconds, if there is a real need in the colony. For example, if there is a sudden need for a large quantity of water to cool the hive, bees will be diverted from other tasks to do this job. Likewise, many bees may engage in ventilating, fanning their wings to move volumes of air through the hive, both to evaporate water to cool the hive and to evaporate excess moisture from freshly gathered nectar. Another example of the bees' ability to change jobs rapidly is seen when a large number of bees are required to defend the colony.

When a worker emerges from her cell, she first engorges on pollen and nectar. Following this, she engages in cleaning cells, perhaps even the one from which she herself emerged. This is in preparation for further egg laying by the queen, or in anticipation of cells being needed for honey storage. The worker's next activity is that of feeding honey and pollen to the older larvae within the hive. This is followed by feeding the younger larvae; since young larvae consume royal jelly, a special food secreted from glands in the heads of worker bees, these glands must be given time to develop after emergence of the worker from her cell, and so there is some delay before this particular task is undertaken. The number of days the worker spends feeding brood depends upon the quantity of brood to be fed and also the pressure for other tasks to be undertaken within the hive.

Following brood feeding, worker bees may engage in comb building and cell capping (the capping of cells containing larvae or those filled with honey). At this time the worker may also engage in taking food from the field bees. Field bees do not place the nectar they collect directly into cells, but rather give it to house bees, who manipulate it further, adding enzymes and aiding in the reduction of moisture. The last task often, but not always, undertaken by a house bee before she becomes a field bee is that of guarding the hive. A worker bee is usually 18 to 21 days of age when this occurs. At this time her sting glands contain the maximum amount of venom, so she makes an ideal guard. A worker bee remains a guard usually less than a day or two.

If all goes well, at about three weeks of age a house bee becomes a field bee. She will not again undertake household tasks unless there is a drastic need for her to do so; however, research shows that she retains the ability to do several tasks, except that of secreting special food from her head glands, which have probably atrophied by this time. (It is also questionable whether old bees can again secrete wax.) As a field bee, the worker engages in the collection of nectar, pollen, water, or propolis, again depending upon the needs within the colony. At this time in her life the worker bee undergoes the greatest stress. Infrequently, a bee will remain out all evening if she happens to be working late at night and is chilled; this can place a great stress on her body. Similarly, winds can fray and tear her wings. There are always other insects and birds that prey upon her as she moves from one flower to another.

Work within the colony never ceases. There is never a time when the whole colony sleeps, but, if you watch individual bees, it is evident that they do rest periodically throughout the day. This is especially true of house bees and less true of field bees; presumably the field bees rest most of the night. You will also note that a single bee spends a great deal of time walking over the comb, as though she is looking for work to be done. For example, rarely will you see a worker bee completely cap a cell of honey or a brood cell by herself. Rather, the capping of a single cell is done by several bees that happen upon the cell and recognize that something must be done about it. It is presumed that this apparently random movement of bees around and through the hive is part of the system that alerts the bees to the work that needs to be done.

## LIFE HISTORY OF THE DRONE

Many people have searched in vain to find some activity, other than mating, for which the drone can be credited. It has been suggested that a large number of drones on the outside of a cluster in the spring helps to insulate it and protect the brood, but if this is so—and it is unlikely—the function is accidental. The drone's whole body is adapted for his sole function. He has no sting or any of the other special body modifications that aid the worker in her role.

Drones are not present in the honey bee colony in the winter. The production of drones starts when the first spring flowers appear. This is in January in the South and April in the North or in between in the middle states. The number of drones peak about three months later in each case. There may be as many as 3,000 drones in a colony, but even a populous colony is more likely to have 1,000 to 1,500.

Drones cease to be fed in the fall and finally, when they are starved and weakened, they are dragged from the hive by worker bees. Contrary to popular notions, not all of the drones are driven from the hive at the same time in the fall. Rather, it appears that the older drones die first, and a very small number of drones persist even after the first frost.

Young drones that have just emerged from their cells feed on honey. However, drones soon learn to solicit food from workers and become very adept at doing so. Old drones, even when they are starving in the fall, have apparently lost the ability to feed themselves and continue to solicit food from workers, even though they are unsuccessful in doing so.

Drones become sexually mature at about 10 to 12 days of age. At this time they begin to take short orientation flights and, later, the longer flights required for searching for their mates. Both virgin queens and drones fly only in the afternoon, thus increasing the chances that the sexes will meet for mating. Drones, and presumably virgin queens, fly to what are called "drone congregation areas," where mating takes place.

A queen mates with several drones. Drones die in the mating process. Proportionally to its body size, the genitalia of a drone are among the very largest of any animal on earth. They are contained within the abdomen and, presumably, getting them out of the abdomen for the purpose of mating places such a strain on the drone that it dies in the process.

No one has ever captured a queen honey bee outside of a hive on a flower, and there are only a few records of anyone ever having captured a drone on a flower. In all of these cases the drones were found on goldenrod flowers in late fall and were presumably old, starving drones. Their presence on goldenrod flowers was probably accidental, and there is no indication that they were feeding. It is an interesting fact, however, that queens and drones feed only within the colony and apparently never in

*The raised capped cells are drone pupae in worker cells, a sign of an old queen that has exhausted her sperm.*

their normal life alight to rest or feed in the field. This means, too, that queen and drone flights are of limited duration, since more food is required for flying. Queen and drone flights average about 20 minutes, rarely much longer.

## LIFE HISTORY OF THE QUEEN

A queen honey bee is a special animal. A queen is important to the colony for two reasons: she lays all the eggs, and she produces secretions from glands in her body that are responsible for the maintenance of social order.

Biologists interested in development and nutrition have pointed to the queen as an example of how food may make tremendous differences in an animal. Queens are fed lavishly by worker bees, as witnessed by the tremendous amount of royal jelly (a thick, white, creamy material) that is found in the base of the cell in which a queen is reared. Queens are markedly different from worker bees. Some of the more apparent morphological differences include the fact that the queen has no wax glands, her sting is lightly barbed and curved, and she has no pollen baskets on her hind legs or other modifications on the forelegs as does the worker. While she has certain of the head glands found in worker bees, these secrete radically different materials. Perhaps most important, the ovaries of the queen are much better developed than those of the worker bee; a queen has a *spermatheca*, a sac in which sperm obtained from mating with drones is stored for long periods of time, even years. By contrast, a worker bee is incapable of mating or storing sperm.

Queen honey bees have been known to live as long as five or six years, though in commercial practice colonies are usually requeened after one or two years. The long life of the queen is important for the continued existence of the colony, since natural queen replacement is a delicate operation whose failure can cause the loss of the entire colony.

Queens are reared only when a colony is about to swarm, when a queen is old and failing and is superseded by a younger queen, and when, for some reason, the colony becomes queenless. When a colony becomes queenless, the honey bees detect the loss of their queen, usually within a few hours, and immediately begin to enlarge the cell around an egg or a one-day-old worker larva in the colony. They then begin to construct a special queen cell in which to rear a new queen.

*Eggs deposited by a queen are upright and in the center of a cell.*

When a queen first emerges from her cell, she is not recognized by the workers as being a queen. The workers pay little attention to her at first, and it is several days before she begins to produce her queen secretions. A virgin queen, upon emergence from her cell, engorges herself on pollen and nectar as does an emerging worker bee. Following this, the queen seeks out other virgin queens and fights and attempts to kill them. If other virgin queens are not present, she turns her attention to other queen cells and destroys them.

A queen honey bee leaves the colony on only two occasions: when she is mating and when she accompanies a swarm. Mating takes place when the queen is five or six days old. About half of the queens mate on their first flight, but some take an orientation flight prior to mating. Queens mate with an average of about 15 to 18 drones in a matter of one or two days, and start to lay eggs two or three days later. From these several matings a queen obtains in the vicinity of 5 million sperm, which will last her the rest of her life. Queens are incapable of mating after they are about three or four weeks old, and old queens that have exhausted their sperm produce eggs that develop only into drones.

Within the colony, the queen is always surrounded by a few worker bees who lick and groom her and feed her. A single worker usually remains with the queen only a few minutes.

Knowing when a queen should be replaced is important in practical beekeeping. Old queens have fewer body hairs and sometimes a black, shiny appearance. The number of worker bees surrounding an old queen is smaller than the number surrounding a young queen, because the old queen is not so attractive to the workers in her hive. However, the easiest way to determine a queen's effectiveness is to check her brood pattern. A young, vigorous queen lays eggs in a compact area in the brood nest. As she grows older, more and more cells in the brood area will be left without eggs. Brood in adjacent cells should be of a similar age; if not, either the queen is not laying in all cells or her eggs are not hatching.

## LIFE HISTORY OF THE COLONY

Colonies of honey bees undergo what beekeepers call a "cycle of the year." In all parts of the northern hemisphere the queen lays the least number of eggs in October and November. It is normal for colonies in Florida and even the far North to start rearing brood in late December and January; however, the quantity will vary because of temperature limitations. This coincides with the time of year that the day length (photoperiod) is increasing, and it has been suggested that an increasing day length is one factor that controls egg laying by the queen and brings about an increased population in the spring. In this regard, it is interesting to note that, when the days start to shorten in late June, the colony division or swarming becomes less of a problem. However, this is only a theory based on casual observation of bee behavior; final proof to demonstrate the factors that control egg laying and colony development is wanting.

In the southernmost states, colony populations can begin to increase in late January as a result of the egg laying in December and early January. In the more northern states and Canada, colonies reach their low population of the year in late January and February. This is because in the northern states, the egg-laying rate is not sufficient to keep pace with the death rate at this time of the year.

Across the southern states colonies reach their peak populations in March, while in the North the peak populations are reached in late June and July. In the northern states it is not uncommon for colonies to have a low populations of 10,000 to 15,000 bees in February and a peak population of 60,000 bees in July. Across the North, colony populations may drop in late July and show a slight population increase again in August when goldenrod and other late summer and fall plants provide the pollen and nectar needed to stimulate brood rearing.

It is because colonies of honey bees show these seasonal variations that many people have suggested we should consider the whole colony as a single animal. This argument has considerable merit, since none of the individuals in the colony can live alone and there must be a sharing of the work for the colony to survive. Furthermore, in the spring the colony shows an increase in population or growth that is somewhat akin to the growth of other animals. At the same time, when the colony suffers from disease, usually all the members of the colony are affected, and one cannot treat individuals separately in most instances. It is important for all beekeepers to determine when changes are taking place in colonies in their area. These changes are determined by the time of year, the weather, and the food available to the colony. Once you understand the cycle of the year in your area, you will be in a position to develop and institute a sound management program.

## COMMUNICATION AND THE SENSES

When many individuals live together in a group, they must have some method whereby they can communicate with one another. Honey bees in a colony face many of the same problems humans face in their society. They must be able to recognize one another and their queen. They must be able to alert one another to danger. When food is found in the field, it is important to tell other members of their community where it is. Within the hive, tasks must be done in an orderly fashion. Thus, the need for an efficient communication system is evident.

In the case of people, speech is the most important form of communication. Visual cues, physical movements, and odors are important, too, but much less so than talking. Honey bees are different. They have an acute sense of smell, far better than we do. As for taste, honey bees can taste about the same things that we can taste insofar as sweet and sour, bitter and salty are concerned. Color is also important to the honey bee, though the bee does not see quite the same range and gradation of colors that we do.

Honey bees use chemical substances, especially in the form of odors, to give information to one another. Chemical substances that convey messages from one member of a community to another are called *pheromones*, a term that was coined in the late 1950s. In precise terminology a pheromone is a chemical substance secreted from a gland in one animal that brings about a specific behavioral response in another individual of the same species.

In the case of the honey bee, several pheromones have been discovered. The roles that certain of these chemical substances play are known and are discussed below. Honey bees use their antennae to detect odors. Microscopic examination of the honey bee's antennae reveals that they are covered with a great number and variety of sensory receptors.

### Sight

Honey bees see four colors distinctly: yellow, blue-green, blue, and ultraviolet. People can distinguish about 60 colors distinctly. Red, on one end of the color spectrum, is perceived as black by bees; on the opposite end of the spectrum bees see ultraviolet, which we cannot see.

Bees do not see designs as well as humans do. For example, bees will confuse a 2-inch circle and a 2-inch square of the same color, but they are able to tell the difference between a solid circle of one color and a circle with only an outline of the same color.

Experiments to determine the colors and designs honey bees see were performed by Professor Karl von Frisch several years ago and are simple to duplicate. One of his experiments involved training bees to go to a feeding station in the field. The feeding station was placed on a small table painted blue or that had a blue piece of cardboard immediately underneath it. After scout bees had made several round trips from the hive to the feeding station, von Frisch would offer the bees a choice of two, three, or four stations close together, but only one of which was marked with blue. Under these circumstances most of the bees alighted at the feeding station that carried the proper color and did so without hesitation.

Another experiment involved training bees to feed at a station inside a colored box with only a small hole leading to the outside. Again, after a suitable training period, the bees would be offered two, three, or four boxes of similar size but colored differently. And again, in this experiment, the bees entered the box marked with the color to which they had been trained. The same experiments may be used to show the shapes and designs bees see distinctly.

Color and design are obviously important in the life of the bee. Once a bee finds a good source of food in the field, it is important that she be able to move from a flower of one kind to another flower of the same kind. The bee does so by using the color and design of the flower. Odor is also important and is discussed below. Insofar as practical beekeeping is concerned, and as is mentioned elsewhere in this text, painting bee hives that are in close proximity to one another different colors helps bees to distinguish their own hive from others in the apiary.

Do bees have a favorite color insofar as flowers are concerned? And, are certain colors better than others for painting hives? Researchers avoid these questions because sight alone is not a dominating factor. Bees use color and probably prefer yellow to other colors, which may explain why so many pollens are yellow or yellow-orange. However, when bees work on flowers they are also concerned with odor and design. If a flower, no matter how attractive its color may be, does not live up to their expectations and provide a good supply of pollen and/or nectar, they move on rapidly. In a similar vein, no one hive color is best everywhere. Light colored hives are probably best in the southern states to help the bees cope with high temperatures. Likewise, darker colors, even black or red, may be more suitable in the north. Many beekeepers paint their individual boxes (supers) different colors, which probably aids the bees in finding their own hive when there is a long row of hives side by side.

### *Odor*

As he had done with color and design, Professor von Frisch investigated the ability of the worker honey bee to detect odors. The design was simple, and the experiments are easily repeated; they demonstrate very clearly that honey bees detect odors.

Professor von Frisch placed scented foods in boxes with only a small entrance. When the bees had been trained to the scented box, they were offered a choice of several boxes, but only one contained the proper odor; the bees entered the correct box without hesitation. It was shown further that honey bees detect odors with their antennae. A worker honey bee's antenna has 12 segments. If the terminal eight segments are removed from one antenna and the terminal seven segments from the second, the bee can still detect an odor. If a terminal eight segments are removed from both antennae, however, the bee is unable to detect odors, indicating that the most important sensory receptors lie on the terminal eight segments.

It was logical to ask next which might be more important, color or odor. When Professor von Frisch trained bees to feeding stations on the bases of both color and odor, he learned that the bees used color from a great distance, but failed to enter the experimental feeding station or to feed if the food was not properly scented.

### *Taste*

Honey bees can detect sweet, sour, salt, and bitter. If, for example, salt is added to a sweet sugar syrup in too great a quantity, the bees will reject the syrup. Interestingly, however, honey bees cannot detect all the tastes that

we can. For example, bees do not taste quinine, and one may add quinine to a sugar syrup, which would taste extremely bitter to humans, but which bees will continue to feed on without hesitation.

Honey bees have a threshold of perception and also a threshold of acceptance. They are able to detect very low sugar concentrations, but they will feed on them only when nothing else is available. Thus, in the field, scout bees have a tendency to work the richer sources of nectar first. As a practical example, there is the problem of pollinating pears in the United States. Pears produce nectar that contains only 10 to 15 percent sugar, while apples, dandelions, and other weeds that flower at the same time usually have a richer sugar concentration in their nectar. As a result, growers do various things, including eliminating competition such as dandelions, in order to have their pears properly pollinated.

### *Pheromones*

The idea that chemical substances exchanged by individuals within the colony might have something to do with social order was first suggested in the 1940s and 1950s. However, it was not until 1961 that the first of these complicated chemical substances was isolated and synthesized so that controlled laboratory experiments could be made. Dr. C. G. Butler of the Rothamsted Experimental Station in England and his colleagues were the first to identify *queen substance*, the name given a group of closely related chemicals. In the colony, this mixture of material is said to have several functions. Queen substance is the material by which honey bees recognize their queen; it inhibits queen replacement, and, so long as the queen is present and producing her secretions, the bees will not build queen cells; it is also thought that queen substance inhibits ovary development in worker bees. The source of queen substance is the queen's mandibular glands. However, when the mandibular glands of a living queen are removed, the worker bees within the colony are still able to recognize her, though to a much lesser extent. Therefore, it is clear that secondary substances also play roles in queen recognition.

Queen substance is the material that causes honey bees to surround, lick, and antennate (groom) their queen. You can place queen substance (synthetic or natural) on a piece or wood or other object, and observe that worker bees will surround and lick it. The fact that honey bees do this

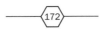

*This beekeeper holds a caged queen in her hand. The worker bees are attracted to the queen because of her pheromones.*

clearly demonstrates they are not fully conscious animals but are merely responding to stimuli in their environment.

It was discovered that queen substance is also the honey bee sex attractant. It is interesting to note that inside the hive drones pay no attention to queens; mating always takes place outside of the hive, and usually at a height greater than 20 feet. Again, experimentally you can use the synthetic queen substance to attract drones by placing it on a wad of cotton, a piece of wood, or some other object and then suspending it from a helium-filled balloon. When this is done, there is clear evidence that the drones, too, are responding to an odor only and that they do not recognize the queen as a living animal.

The fact that chemical substances can play so many roles in a honey bee colony is perhaps not surprising. In the course of evolution, animals have usually found the most efficient way of communicating and maintaining social order.

Isoamyl acetate is the alarm odor in honey bees. This chemical substance, secreted from the vicinity of the worker honey bee's sting, alerts other bees to danger and causes them to attack. Interestingly enough, this

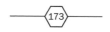

honey bee alarm odor is a common chemical that has been on laboratory shelves for years, but no one had ever thought of testing it as such. As with queen substance, a very small quantity of the synthetic material dropped in the vicinity of the hive will cause bees to attack and sting.

It is also a fact that honey bees will attack as a result of the release of alarm odor only in the vicinity of their hive. Perhaps this is logical, for it is the colony and not themselves that they are trying to protect. If alarm odor is released in the vicinity of a worker bee in the field, she will flee, because in the field there is nothing for her to defend except herself.

There is a second alarm substance in honey bees, which is secreted from the worker's mandibular glands. Presumably it is with this material that worker honey bees may also mark an enemy. In any event, it is no accident that honey bees are able to follow an enemy. It is fairly certain that the reason that a sting is left in a victim by a honey bee is for the precise purpose of marking the enemy, as the alarm odor will continue to be released no matter where the enemy flees.

*A worker bee exposes her scent gland in this picture. The scent gland pheromone flows to the right as a result of the wing fanning.*

Worker honey bees mark food sources and, under certain circum-stances, their own hive or a new nest by exposing the scent gland on the tip of their abdomen. Four chemicals are released at the same time from this gland. As might be imagined, an individual scent gland on a worker honey bee secretes a very small quantity of scent, and the identification of the materials involved a remarkable piece of chemical sleuthing.

From this research, it is clear that there are many pheromones that control other aspects of social order in the honey bee colony. Investigators in many parts of the world are exploring the honey bee community in order to identify these substances and the roles they play. Since the quanti-ties of the materials involved are small, the research is slow and tedious and demands the use of sophisticated chemical apparatus.

### The dance language

Perhaps the most fascinating aspect of honey bee biology is the dances worker bees perform to tell other bees in the hive about food sources in the field. There are basically two types of dance, the round dance and the wag-tail dance, both involving physical movements, yet each conveying very definite messages. What is most intriguing about the dances of the honey bee is that we can "read" them, but we do not know how honey bees do so. Research shows that worker honey bees must follow several dancing bees in order to understand the message conveyed in the dance. However, not all of the bees that follow dancing bees and leave the hive necessarily locate the food source.

The early research on the dance language of the honey bee was undertaken almost exclusively by one man and his students, Professor Karl von Frisch of Germany. Professor von Frisch began working with honey bees as early as 1914, but it was not until the late 1940s that he came to understand the honey bee dances. The basic von Frisch experiments have been repeated by many people and are now routinely used in laboratories to demonstrate this form of animal communication.

More than just physical movements are used to convey information about food sources in the field to bees that are being recruited by scouts. A scout bee that has found a rich source of nectar will also pause fre-quently and give a taste of the nectar to a potential recruit. In doing so, the recruit is able to perceive the sugar concentration of the food and also to determine its odor. If the food source is located close to the hive, odor from the flowers in which the bees have worked in collecting their nectar clings to the outside of their bodies (on their hair) and is detected by recruits.

Precisely the same dances are used to convey information about pollen and, to a much lesser extent, propolis and water when these items are needed in the hive. While it is clear how scout bees convey information that the item to be collected is nectar or water by giving a taste of it to recruit bees, it is not at all clear how they convey information about the fact that it is pollen or propolis. This mystery remains to be researched by some thorough, careful investigator. When honey bee colonies swarm, the same dances are used to indicate a new home site. Again, how scouts communicate to other bees that it is a home site that is being danced about is not at all clear; what is clear is that the proper message is conveyed to the bees in a swarm, for experimentally it can be shown that they move to the new site without hesitation.

The simplest of the honey bee dances is the round dance. The round dance indicates to recruit bees that food is to be found within about a hundred yards of the hive and that they should go out and search for it. Von Frisch proved this point by setting up a feeding station within a hundred yards of a hive and trained a certain number of scouts to go to it. These scouts were marked so that they could later be differentiated from the recruits that came to the feeding station. After a training period, the original station was removed and four feeding stations were set up at cardinal points of the compass at an equal distance from the hive. The bees that visited each of these stations were then counted, and it was found that the bees came in about equal numbers to all four feeding stations. This was not the case, however, when scouts danced the wag-tail dance.

Certain races of bees use a dance intermediate between the round dance and the wag-tail dance incorporating parts of both. Such a dance is used to indicate distances of usually 50 to about 100 yards. This intermediate dance was not discovered by Professor von Frisch, for the race of bees he was using experimentally did not perform this dance. This demonstrates the kind of biological variation that can exist even among animals of the same species, and it should serve to warn all investigators of the kinds of experimental error that can be made.

Perhaps the most interesting of the honey bee dances is the wag-tail dance, which conveys to recruits information about the direction and distance of the food source from the hive. The dance is remarkably simple and may be followed by anyone using a glass-walled observation hive. The fact that so much information can be conveyed by a dance is remarkable.

The rapidity with which the dance is performed by a scout bee indicates the distance of the food source from the hive. For experimental purposes, Professor von Frisch chose to count the number of completed dances within a 15-second period. He placed this information on a graph and showed that when food sources were close to the hive, the bees were more excited and danced more rapidly. When food sources were at greater distances,, the scouts danced more slowly. Just as we may show enthusiasm by the rapidity of our movements, so, apparently, honey bees use the "enthusiasm" of their dance to indicate the closeness of a food source. It is thus clear that if two bees are dancing side by side and one indicates a food source close to the hive, while another indicates a food source farther away, recruits will be more attracted to the bee dancing more rapidly.

The inside of the hive is dark. The part of the dance made when the bee is running the wag-tail itself indicates the direction of the food from the hive as oriented by the sun. In the hive, the worker honey bee transforms sun direction into gravity. Therefore, if a bee dances directly up on a comb, she is indicating that the source of the food lies in the direction of the sun. If the same bee dances directly down, she is indicating to recruits "go away from the sun" to find food. The direction of the dance changes during the day as the sun moves across the sky.

Again, in what has become a classic experiment, Professor von Frisch showed the accuracy of the wag-tail dance with ease. After training bees to a food source in the field for a given period of time, he established a series of feeding stations on both sides of the original station and then began to count the number of recruits that appeared at all stations. He found that a remarkably large number of bees arrived at the original station, but that a small number of bees came to the feeding stations on either side of the station to which the scouts had been trained. The fact that bees can find the feeding station at all under these circumstances is remarkable, yet it is clear why there might be some variation. Under normal circumstances a scout bee dances to indicate a clump of flowers or a tree from which

recruits might gather food, or, more commonly, to indicate a field or a forest in flower. In fact, were there not an abundance of food in the field, the scout bee would not have been sufficiently enthused to dance at all.

One other factor that influences the enthusiasm with which scout bees dance is the way in which their food is received in the hive. Bees that have collected nectar do not deposit it in cells themselves but rather give it to house bees. If a scout bee is unable to find a house bee to take her food because they are all busy, she is much less inclined to dance and/or she dances for a shorter period of time. If the scout bee cannot find cells within the hive in which to deposit pollen, she is much less inclined to dance to indicate a pollen source.

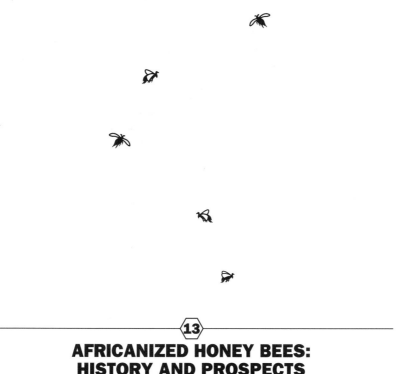

---

# 13

# AFRICANIZED HONEY BEES: HISTORY AND PROSPECTS

I N 1956, PROFESSOR WARWICK E. KERR BROUGHT SEVERAL queen honey bees from Africa to his laboratory in Brazil. Most of these were from a queen breeder's apiary a few miles south of the South African capital city of Pretoria. Kerr had the support of the Brazilian government and beekeepers in this project. At the time, there was a thriving beekeeping industry in the southern, cooler part of Brazil using European honey bees in the same way that we do in North America. However, in the hot, humid north of Brazil, especially the Amazon River Basin, the European bees could not survive.

It was Kerr's aim to bring into Brazil tropical bees that could cope

*Bees will occupy any cavity of the proper size. Here they have entered a squirrel nest box.*

with a tropical climate. The African bees escaped before the breeding project was completed and bred with local bees. However, the goal outlined by Kerr was achieved. African bees form the basis of a successful beekeeping industry in Brazil today.

There has been a beekeeping industry throughout Africa for thousands of years. While primitive, and using nonmovable frame hives, the several countries making up East Africa often export as much beeswax annually as is produced in the United States, thus testifying to the size of the industry. The fact that African bees are more aggressive was well known long before Kerr's Africans escaped in Brazil. Having worked with these bees in Africa, I am very much aware that African beekeepers do not keep their bees in their villages, but rather in locations scattered across the countryside.

## THE POLITICS OF AFRICANIZED HONEY BEES

Politics entered the picture in 1964 when the military took control of Brazil's government. Professor Kerr did not care for the military government and said so. Kerr was well known in scientific and government circles and was often needed by his government to represent them at conferences abroad. Even a dictatorial, military government must have some contacts with the outside world. Thus, Kerr, unlike many of his colleagues who were imprisoned for long periods of time, spent only two nights in jail for his opposition during the nearly 20-year military reign in Brazil.

Kerr's outspokenness was a problem for his local military commander. However, even the military did not dare to enter the church where Kerr was a Sunday school teacher and spoke against the government.

Africanized honey bees are more aggressive than European honey bees, and there were some stinging incidents reported. To discredit Kerr locally, the military made a number of news releases blaming all stinging problems, whether they were caused by yellow jackets, bumble bees, wasps, or honey bees, on Kerr. In a military situation, when the government controls and censors the press, a person such as Kerr has no opportunity to reply.

The first mention of the words "killer bees" in the United States was on September 24, 1965, when *Time* magazine recapped one of these local press releases and translated the term from Portuguese, the language of Brazil. The name stuck. *Time* ran a second, similar story in 1967. The killer bee story has been headline news ever since whenever there is peace and quiet on earth and little else in the horror line for the press to write about. There have been five books, as many movies, and an endless number of newspaper and magazine articles—almost all of them presenting a decidedly one-sided and inaccurate account of the story.

## WHAT ARE AFRICANIZED HONEY BEES?

Today, there is a thriving beekeeping industry in tropical and subtropical Brazil using hybrids between the European and African honey bees. In the warmer regions, the bees are predominantly African, while further south in the temperate areas of the country, they are more European. We call all of these bees "Africanized" to differentiate them from African bees. These bees are not a new species or race of honey bees. They are a mixture of several European and African races.

In the tropical areas of South America, the Africanized bees of Brazil are about 97 percent African. As we move away from the equator they tend to become more Europeanized. In the temperate region of Argentina—an

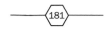

*These are queen mating nuclei in a shaded mating apiary in central Brazil.*

area whose climate resembles the central and northern United States—where it is cooler and apples, for example, are an important crop, the European genetic material dominates. It is important to understand that there is great variation among Africanized honey bees.

Interestingly, African and Africanized honey bees are about 10 percent smaller than European bees. Their smaller size is one of the ways by which they are identified. Their sting and the associated venom glands are smaller, too. Tests conducted with their venom show it to be no different from that of European honey bees.

So what is the problem? The answer is that, on average and when they are aroused, there are more stinging bees per colony in the case of Africanized honey bees. Also, our observations show that African and Africanized honey bees will pursue anyone who disturbs their nest for a longer distance than European bees. However, those of us who work with European bees are also aware that every so often we find a colony, and sometimes a whole apiary, where the bees are more aggressive than normal, and even African-like in their behavior. There are several factors that cause even European honey bees to be more aggressive, including a shortage of food in the field and inclement and/or warm weather. Bees in colonies that are being disturbed by skunks, or by humans, who may be inspecting a colony every day in an experimental situation, may act unusually defensive and agressive.

## ARE AFRICANIZED HONEY BEES DANGEROUS?

All stinging insects can be dangerous. Persons concerned with public health have always emphasized that bees, wasps, hornets, and other stinging insects should not be allowed to nest where they can become a nuisance. There are two factors to consider in the case of all stinging insects. Some people suffer from stings because they are allergic, and others because they receive a large dose of venom. One should be careful and exercise some common sense with all stinging insects. For example, you should never walk in a honey bee or wasp colony's flight path, no matter what their origin.

Brazilian beekeepers use larger smokers and more protective clothing than most North American beekeepers when working their bees because their bees are more aggressive. Beekeepers in Brazil also select the locations for their apiaries with care and do their best to keep bees away from people and animals—but, then, so do beekeepers in North America. However, the horror stories about "killer bees" that were reported early on from Brazil have not been heard from Africa, and now that Brazil has once again returned to a civilian government, similar stories are seldom heard there anymore.

Unfortunately, there have always been unpleasant stinging incidents wherever honey bees are kept, just as there are wherever any animals exist. The United States bee journals, long before Africanized bees existed, have often reported instances in which large animals have died as a result of excessive stinging. Horses, for example, have been known to wander into an apiary, be stung, kick at the nearest hive, and be stung again and again until they die. Some Brazilian beekeepers fence their apiaries, but most do not.

## PREDICTING THE FUTURE

On October 15, 1990 a natural swarm of Africanized bees was found in the southernmost part of Texas, where it had migrated from Mexico. These

bees have since moved into other states. They will continue to spread.

It is not difficult to predict what will happen as Africanized honey bees spread across the United States. We have only to look at Brazil, Argentina, and Mexico to learn. In the southern states the bees will be more African and more aggressive. In the northern United States and Canada they will be less so.

We know that in Africa and in Central and South America Africanized honey bees are good honey producers. In fact, many beekeepers in Brazil who have worked with both groups prefer the Africans. Africanized honey bees are different from European bees but we have the experience of beekeepers from the whole of Central and South America on which to build.

There are migratory beekeepers in several countries in South America. Beekeepers grow queens from these bees using the same techniques we use in this country. No one has complained about a shortage of bees for pollination where the Africanized honey bees exist. Africanized honey bees are more aggressive, but they can be managed. Being forewarned, we dress and behave accordingly.

## NEW VILLAGE AND TOWN ORDINANCES

Many cities, towns, and villages prohibit the keeping of most animals within their boundaries. However, increasingly, we are hearing about special ordinances that are being enacted to prevent beekeeping in residential areas. What many people do not realize is that, wherever there are flowering plants producing pollen and nectar, there will be bees.

The most effective, and perhaps the only way to eliminate honey bees or other stinging insects from an area, is to remove their food sources. This includes removing flowering plants that are attractive to honey bees because of the pollen and/or nectar they produce. There are some flowers that produce no pollen or nectar, for example, garden roses. (Wild roses, on the other hand, are usually attractive to honey bees.)

A few years ago we surveyed the upstate New York city of Oswego for colonies of honey bees living in trees, houses, and human-kept hives. We found 12 colonies in the 1.6 square miles occupied by the city. Only one was in a human-made hive; the rest were found living in trees and buildings. Oswego is an old city, and there is an abundance of flowering plants, especially white Dutch clover, in lawns. Our data show that an ordinance will not reduce the number of honey bee colonies in a city area. One might logically ask whether it is better to have wild colonies living unsupervised where the bees prefer, or to have colonies under the control of beekeepers and inspectors?

## HOW DO AFRICANIZED HONEY BEES DOMINATE?

African and Africanized bees develop in a shorter period of time than other types of honey bees. Africanized queens, for example, may emerge from their cells almost a day earlier than their European counterparts. When a colony is growing queens, which it does when it is swarming or replacing its queen, it raises several queens at the same time. The first queen to emerge in a colony kills the others. This is a natural rule: there can be only one queen in a hive. Thus, queens with African genetic material have the advantage when they are reared together with European bees. This is probably the chief factor that has given them an advantage over local bees as they have migrated north from Brazil and into this country.

Swarms of Africanized bees fly long distances, perhaps a hundred or more miles. We know from observations in Mexico that a typical swarm settles in midafternoon, and the workers forage then and in the following morning—"tanking up," so to speak. They fly as long as they have food (fuel) to keep them airborne, and then they settle and forage again. It is true that European honey bees, introduced into North America in the 1600s, moved across much of the United States more rapidly than did the European settlers, but we have no precise data as to how fast they traveled or how they did it.

The fact we do know and understand, however, is that Africanized honey bees will move across the southern United States quite rapidly. Their movement may be speeded up by modern agriculture, which requires bees for pollination. Over 1 million colonies of honey bees are moved east and west, north and south, for pollination each year. Many colonies are also moved for honey production.

## SWARMING AND ABSCONDING

It has been reported that Africanized honey bees swarm more frequently than European bees. It has also been stated that they abscond (abandon the

This is a natural, migrating swarm of Africanized bees settling in a bush in the late afternoon. The swarm will move again in the morning after the bees have foraged and built up their reserve of food.

hive) more rapidly. Both of these statements are partially correct. However, Brazilian beekeepers have had considerable experience as regards both of these differences, and we can learn from them. There is also great variation insofar as both of these qualities are concerned. The cause of swarming is congestion in all races of bees. It is therefore important that beekeepers prevent congestion. This is done by giving colonies additional space. It is also true that if colonies of Africanized honey bees run out of food they may abscond. It is therefore important to make certain that they always have some food.

## DO AFRICANIZED HONEY BEES HAVE ANY SPECIAL QUALITIES?

One may find both critics and defenders of these new bees. Africanized honey bees have several virtues. There is no question that they are excellent honey producers in warm climates. They are likewise excellent pollinators.

Africanized honey bees are good housekeepers and defenders of their nests. They are naturally resistant, through grooming, to the worst of all of the honey bee diseases caused by the mite, *Varroa jacobsoni*. This mite was accidently introduced into Paraguay and subsequently Brazil in the early 1970s. We find varroa mites in every colony when we search for them in Brazil. Yet Brazilian beekeepers pay little attention to the mites, and no one treats his colonies because of varroa. While a few colonies of bees of European stock in the United States have some degree of resistance to the mites, it is more pronounced in the Africanized bees.

We can requeen colonies of Africanized honey bees with European stock, though it is not easy to do so. In South America some beekeepers keep both races of bees in the same apiary.

The introduction of Africanized honey bees into the United States will have some effect on the industry and on those who keep bees, ranging from hobbyists to commercial beekeepers. However, we have had a long experience with bees of all races, and both we and the bees will adapt.

## RESEARCH AND QUESTIONS

We know several interesting facts about Africanized honey bee behavior. Africanized colonies are less aggressive in cooler climates. When colonies of Africanized honey bees were moved south in Brazil to a temperate climate, they became less aggressive. Moving Africanized bees to higher elevations also modifies their behavior, making them calmer. The few beekeepers in Africa who have used bee houses (houses in which colonies are kept and where the colony entrances face outdoors only) state that it is easier to control the bee's behavior in a bee house. It has been suggested that the bee houses keep the colonies cooler and thereby have an advantage.

All of the beekeeping advice that has been given during the past 100 years is increasingly important. For example, bees should be kept in isolated areas or behind hedgerows and fences that force them to fly high and above the heads of people. Pets and animals should be kept away from bees. The beekeeper should dress properly when entering an apiary. Learning how to use smoke carefully and effectively is important.

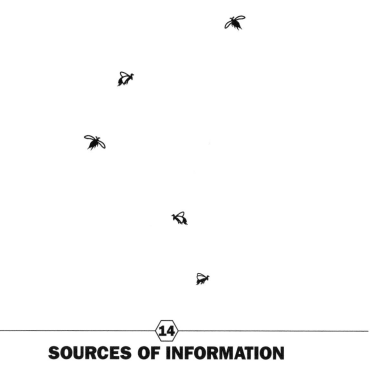

---

## ⟨14⟩
## SOURCES OF INFORMATION

ONLY A FEW ANIMALS HAVE HAD MORE WRITTEN about them than the honey bee. Both historically and in modern times, there is a wealth of information available about bees and beekeeping. There are thousands of books, journals, bulletins, and brochures devoted to bee culture. There are also hundreds of beekeepers organizations, ranging from those on the county and regional level to national and international associations. Still, the best way to learn about honey bees is to work with a commercial or hobby beekeeper who has been keeping bees for a number of years. There is no substitute for hands-on experience.

## THE EXTENSION SERVICE

In 1914, the United States Congress established the Agricultural Extension Service to work in conjunction with the state colleges that had been established previously. The purpose of the Extension Service is to get information about research performed in the state colleges out to farmers and other professional growers, to make agriculture more efficient and food cheaper. Each organized county in the country has an agricultural extension agent(s), who has an office from which information, including that on honey bees, is available. The Extension Service was intended to complement the teaching and research activities of the state colleges.

## THE STATE COLLEGES

Each state has an agricultural college that is supported by a combination of state and federal funds. About half of the state colleges have a specialist working with honey bees, and a few have more than one person. State college professors are usually responsible for teaching and research on honey bees and often are also extension specialists who provide information to the county agents. The extensionists often write bulletins and circulars on bees that are especially valuable because they cover local honey plants and seasonal management. A few have even prepared slide sets and tapes of regional interest.

These written materials may be obtained directly from the state colleges and sometimes from the county agricultural extension agents. Some extension apiculturists will speak at regional and local association meetings. In some states, the extension specialists work with the state fair on exhibits and honey shows.

## THE STATE DEPARTMENTS OF AGRICULTURE

All states have a department of agriculture that is largely a regulatory agency. Because regulators must often act rapidly, and even trespass to enforce rules and regulations, their activities have been kept separate from the functions of the state colleges. About half of the states have a state apiary inspector, whose job it is to oversee the inspection of honey bee colonies for diseases, to approve interstate shipments of bees, and to make recommendations concerning bee disease control. In several states, the office of state apiary inspector has been eliminated, or the funding reduced, in recent years because of a demand to spend tax money on other public services. Increasingly, it is up to beekeepers themselves to diagnose and treat any diseases that may be found in their apiaries.

## THE FEDERAL LABORATORIES

Shortly before the turn of the last century the federal government became engaged in bee research, including the importation of new stock. This program has been expanded and today there are federal bee research laboratories in Beltsville, Maryland, Logan, Utah, Baton Rouge, Louisianna, Tucson, Arizona, and Weslaco, Texas. Each of these laboratores has several persons engaged in research, usually with assigned projects. These researchers may sometimes be engaged in teaching at a local state college and in other local beekeeping affairs.

The Honey Bee Laboratory at the U.S. Department of Agriculture in Beltsville, Maryland will examine samples of dead bees and brood for diseases from anywhere in the world at no charge. The providing of an international service has kept this laboratory up-to-date on world bee disease affairs, which has proven to be in the best interest of all U.S. beekeepers. Samples of brood or bees should be sent in paper (not plastic) packages to the Beneficial Insects Laboratory, BARC-East, Building 476, Beltsville, MD 20705. It might be best to write or phone the laboratory for more specific instructions before sending any material. The laboratory does not examine honey bees for pesticide losses.

## BEE SUPPLY DEALERS

There are several companies that make beekeeping equipment and supplies. Some of these companies have local dealers who are also a valuable source of information. The bee supply dealers usually stock books, and often bulletins and other literature, from the state colleges and the bee equipment manufacturers. They will also know about local beekeepers meetings.

## TRADE JOURNALS

In the United States there are three monthly trade journals, one with a newspaper format, that carry articles on bees and beekeeping:
*American Bee Journal,* Dadant and Sons, Hamilton, Illinois 62341
*Bee Culture,* A. I. Root Co., 623 West Liberty St., Medina, Ohio 44256

*The Speedy Bee,* P.O. Box 998. Jesup, Georgia 31545

All three of the above journals have a space each month devoted to upcoming international, national, state, and local beekeepers meetings.

## THE NATIONAL HONEY BOARD

In 1986, beekeepers in the United States approved a referendum to create The National Honey Board. The board conducts market research and advertises and promotes honey to expand the market. The board's work is financed by an assessment of one cent per pound on all beekeepers who produce more than 6,000 pounds of honey a year. The board consists of 13 members elected from among producers, packers, importers, a cooperative, and the general public. Board members are not compensated for their time but are paid expenses to attend meetings. The current board's address is 421 21st Avenue #203, Longmont, Colorado 80501.

## BEEKEEPERS' MEETINGS AND ORGANIZATIONS

Two national beekeepers organizations meet each year in January to discuss matters of interest to their members. These are the American Beekeeping Federation and the National Honey Producers Association. Additionally, there are several regional organizations, including the Southern States Beekeepers Association, the Eastern Apicultural Society, and the Western Apicultural Association. The last two of these organizations include some Canadian provinces within their meeting area. Each state has its own beekeepers organization and often several local or county clubs. Some of these groups have their own magazines or newsletters. Most of the local, state, regional, and national associations, together with their addresses, are listed annually in the April issue of *Bee Culture* magazine.

## BOOKS

A good library is your best defense against changing times. Many of the books available treat special areas in greater detail than can be printed here. Some of these are as follows:

*ABC and XYZ of Bee Culture.* R.A. Morse and K. Flottum, writers and editors. 40th Edition. A. I. Root Co., Medina, Ohio 44256. 516 pages. 1990.

*The Archeology of Beekeeping.* E. Crane. Cornell University Press, Ithaca, New York 14850. 360 pages. 1983.

*The Hive and the Honey Bee.* J. M. Graham, editor. Dadant and Sons, Hamilton, Illinois 62341. 1,324 pages. 1992.

*Honeybee Ecology.* T. D. Seeley. Princeton University Press, Princeton, New Jersey 09540. 201 pages. 1985.

*Honey Bee Pests, Predators, and Diseases.* R. A. Morse and R. Nowogrodzki, editors. 2nd Edition. Cornell University Press, Ithaca, New York 14850. 474 pages. 1990.

*Honey in the Comb.* E. E. Killion. Dadant and Sons, Hamilton, Illinois 62341. 148 pages. 1981.

*Rearing Queen Honey Bees.* R. A. Morse. 2nd Edition. Wicwas Press, P.O. Box 817. Cheshire, Connecticut 06410. 1994.

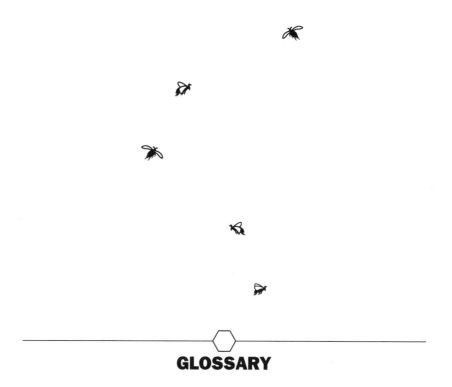

# GLOSSARY

**Abdomen.** The posterior or third region of the body of an insect; in the honey bee it contains the honey stomach, intestines, sting, and reproductive organs.

**Absconding swarm.** A swarm consisting of all the members of a colony that abandons the hive because of wax moth infestation, excessive heat or water, or other causes.

**Africanized honey bee(s).** Descendants of the bees introduced into Brazil from Africa in 1956.

**Afterswarms.** Swarms that leave the hive after the first or primary swarm has departed; afterswarms can be classified as secondary swarms, tertiary swarms, etc.

**Alarm odor.** A chemical substance, released by a worker bee, that alerts other bees to danger.

**Antenna.** One of two long, sensory, segmented filaments located on the head of an insect.

**Apiary.** The sum total of colonies, hives, and other equipment assembled on one site for beekeeping operations.

**Apiculture.** The science and art of raising honey bees.

***Apis mellifera.*** The common honey bee now found throughout the western world, though originally from Europe and Africa. Humans have carried *Apis mellifera* to all continents.

**Bait hive.** A box, usually about the size of a 10-frame Langstroth super, used to attract and capture feral swarms of honey bees.

**Balling a queen.** An attack on a queen by a number of worker bees. In this process the bees form a small cluster or ball of bees around the queen.

**Bee escape.** A device so constructed that bees may pass through in one direction but cannot return. It is used to remove bees from supers or buildings.

**Bee repellent.** A chemical that causes bees to retreat from its point of application. It is used for driving bees out of a hive or part of a hive.

**Bee space.** A space big enough to permit free passage for a bee, but too small to encourage comb building and too large to induce propolization by bees. It measures from ¼ to ⁵⁄₁₆ of an inch.

**Bee tree.** A hollow tree occupied by a colony of bees.

**Bee veil.** A cloth or wire veil for protecting the beekeeper's head and neck from stings.

**Beeswax.** A complex mixture of organic compounds secreted by four pairs of glands on the ventral or underside of the worker bee's abdomen and used by bees for building comb. Its melting point is about 148°F (64° C.).

**Boardman feeder.** A wood or plastic tray that holds a one or two quart jar of sugar syrup, placed at a colony entrance for feeding the bees in the hive.

**Bottomboard.** The floor of a human-made bee hive.

**Box hive.** Any box, used to hive bees, in which the combs are not removable.

**Brace comb.** Small pieces of comb made by bees as connecting links between combs or between a comb and the wall or top of the hive. Also called burr comb.

**Brood.** Immature bees not yet emerged from their cells, i.e., eggs, larvae, and pupae.

**Brood chamber.** That part of a hive in which the brood is reared; the brood chamber may include one or more hive bodies and the combs within.

**Brood nest.** That part of the hive interior in which brood is reared.

**Brood rearing.** The raising of young bees from eggs.

**Capped brood.** Brood whose cells have been sealed by the bees with a wax cover to isolate the immature bees within during their nonfeeding larval and pupal periods.

**Cappings.** The thin wax covering of cells full of honey; also, the same after it has been sliced from the surface of a honey-filled comb that is to be extracted.

**Chilled brood.** Immature bees that have died from excessive cold, usually due to mismanagement by the beekeeper.

**Clipping a queen.** Trimming the wings or wing of a queen to prevent her from flying.

**Cluster.** The form or arrangement in which bees cling together after swarming or during winter.

**Colony.** An aggregate of worker bees, drones, and a queen bee living together in a hive or in any other dwelling as one social unit.

**Comb.** A back-to-back arrangement of two series of hexagonal cells made of wax to hold eggs, brood, pollen, or honey. There are approximately five worker cells to the linear inch and four drone cells to the inch.

**Comb foundation.** A thin sheet of beeswax embossed or stamped with the bases of normal worker cells, on which the bees will construct a complete comb.

**Comb honey.** Honey in the comb, usually produced in small wooden sections measuring $4\frac{1}{4}$" x $4\frac{1}{4}$" or 4" x 5". Round sections have also become popular recently.

**Compound eyes.** The two large lateral eyes of the adult honey bee, composed of many visual elements called ommatidia.

**Deep super.** A super used to hold standard, full-depth frames; the usual depth is $9\frac{5}{8}$ inches.

**Division board.** A thin vertical board of the same length and height as the inside of the hive. It is used to reduce the size of the chamber or to divide the hive into two parts.

**Division board feeder.** A wooden compartment or trough that is hung in a hive like a frame and contains a solution of syrup to feed bees.

**Drawn comb(s).** Comb(s) having the cells built out by honey bees from a sheet of foundation.

**Drifting.** The entering of foreign hives by individual bees that fail to find their own hive after a flight.

**Drone.** The male honey bee.

**Drone brood.** The male brood, reared (in drone comb) in larger cells than worker brood.

**Drone comb.** Comb having cells measuring about four cells to the linear inch. Drone comb has about 18.5 cells to the square inch on each side of the comb.

**Drone layer.** A queen who lays only unfertilized eggs, which result in drones, because she no longer has any sperm, was improperly mated, or was not mated at all.

**Drumming.** A beekeeper's rhythmic pounding on the sides of a hive to drive the bees upward. The method is used in transferring bees from box hives.

**Dry swarm.** A swarm in which the bees have exhausted their food, usually because of inclement weather. Bees in a dry swarm can be aggressive.

**Dysentery.** A condition of adult bees resulting from the accumulation and retention of feces. Usually it occurs only during winter and is caused by unfavorable wintering conditions and low-quality food. Dysentery is detected by small spots of feces around the entrance and within the hive.

**Extracted honey.** Honey removed from combs by means of a centrifugal force machine called an extractor.

**Fertile queen.** A queen that has been inseminated artificially or naturally with drone sperm and is capable of laying fertilized eggs.

**Field bees.** Worker bees, usually 21 or more days old, that work in the field to collect nectar, pollen, water, and/or propolis.

**Finishing colony.** A usually queenright colony into which queen cells that were grafted 24 hours earlier are placed for further care and development.

**Fixed comb.** A comb attached permanently to the wood in a tree or building by a feral colony as opposed to a colony with movable frames.

**Frame.** Four pieces of wood designed to hold honey comb. It consists of one top bar, with or without shoulders, one bottom bar, and two end bars.

**Free-hanging frame.** A frame without shoulders, usually made so that the top bar, end bars, and bottom bar are all the same width.

**Grafting.** The process of removing a worker larva from its cell and placing it in an artificial queen cup to have it reared into a queen.

**Granulation.** A term applied to the process by which honey becomes crystallized, candied, or solidified.

**Guard bees.** Bees, usually about 18 to 21 days in age, that stand at a colony's entrance and watch for strangers, intruders, and robbers.

**Heavy brood foundation.** See Comb foundation; heavy brood foundation is thicker than regular foundation, so there are fewer sheets per pound.

**Hive.** A home for bees provided by beekeepers.

**Hive body.** A human-made box used to hold frames (combs) and house a colony. The dimensions of a Langstroth hive are 16¼" x 20" x 9⅝".

**Hive tool.** A metal device used to open hives, pry frames apart, clean the hive, etc.

**Hoffman frame.** A frame with end bars wide enough at the top to act as a spacing device.

**Honey.** A sweet substance produced by bees by adding enzymes to nectar that they have gathered, and by reducing the moisture content; it is stored in the combs (*Also see Nectar*).

**Honey bee.** The common name for bees in the genus *Apis*. The term is correctly written as two words, though some bee journals and texts cling to the use of "honeybee" (or worse, "honey-bee") as one word.

**Honeydew or honey dew.** A sweet, nectar-like substance secreted by insects such as plant lice or scale insects and sometimes collected by bees. The term can refer to the secretions from extrafloral nectaries, which are nectaries on stems or leaves not associated with flowers.

**Honey flow.** The available nectar supply; loosely, a good supply of nectar. This term is used interchangeably with the term *nectar flow*.

**Innercover.** A lightweight cover used under a standard telescoping cover on a bee hive.

**Instrumental insemination.** The introduction of drone spermatozoa into the genital organs of a virgin queen by special instruments.

**Langstroth frame.** A frame measuring 17⅝" long by 9⅛" deep, exclusive of the lugs or shoulders that support the frame.

**Larva.** The second stage in the development of an insect (such as the honey bee) having complete metamorphosis or four stages: egg, larva, pupa, and adult. (The plural is *larvae*.)

**Laying worker.** A worker bee that lays eggs. Such eggs develop into drones. Laying workers usually develop in colonies that have been queenless for a long period of time.

**Mandibles.** The jaws of an insect. In the honey bee and most other insects the mandibles move in a horizontal rather than in a vertical plane.

**Mating flight.** The flight taken by a virgin queen during which she mates in the air with one or more drones. Normal queens mate 15 to 18 times on two or more mating flights.

**Mating nuc.** A small colony, usually with only one or two thousand worker bees, into which queen cells about to emerge are placed. The young queens will fly and mate from here.

**Migratory beekeeping.** The moving of colonies of bees from one locality to another during a single year, either for plant pollination or so that advantage can be taken of two or more honey flows.

**Movable frame.** A frame or comb that is easily removed from a hive for inspection or manipulation. It is constructed on the principle of "bee space," which prevents it from being attached to its surroundings by pieces of burr comb or heavy deposits of propolis. *See also Bee space.*

**Nasonov gland.** The name given to the gland associated with the upper side of the seventh abdominal tergite of the worker honey bee. This gland is commonly called the *scent gland* and produces an assembly pheromone.

**Natural swarm.** A swarm of bees issuing spontaneously from a parent hive to form a new colony.

**Nectar.** A sweet exudation secreted by glands in different parts of plants, chiefly in the flowers. It is the raw material of which honey is made.

**Nectaries.** The glands of plants that secrete nectar.

**Nuc box.** Any small-size box that is used to house a mating nucleus or any small colony of honey bees.

**Nucleus.** A small colony of bees often used in queen rearing or for holding queens for requeening.

**Observation hive.** A hive made largely of glass to permit observation of the bees at work.

**Ocellus.** A simple eye with a single lens. The honey bee has three ocelli on the topmost portion of the head.

**Package.** A quantity of bees (usually 2 to 5 pounds), with or without a queen, contained in a shipping cage.

**Pheromone.** A chemical substance that is released externally by one animal and that stimulates a specific behavioral response in a second animal of the same species.

**Pollen.** The male reproductive cell bodies of flowers, which are collected and used by bees for rearing their young. It provides the protein in the honey bee's diet.

**Pollen basket.** A flattened depression surrounded by curved spines located on the outside of the tibiae of the bee's hind legs and adapted for carrying the pollen gathered from flowers to the hive. Sometimes termed the *corbicula.*

**Pollen bound.** A term referring to the condition when most of a colony's cells over and alongside the brood nest are filled with pollen; this leaves no place for the queen to lay and thus congests the colony.

**Pollen substitute.** A food material that substitutes completely for pollen in a bee's diet.

**Pollen supplement.** A food material that, mixed with pollen, substitutes for pollen in a bee's diet.

**Pollen trap.** A human-made device for removing pollen from the pollen baskets of bees as they return to their hives.

**Pollination.** The transfer of pollen from the anthers (male parts) to the stigmas (female parts) of flowers.

**Pollinator.** The agent that transmits pollen from one flower to another. Various insects, birds, and mammals function as pollinators.

**Prime swarm.** The first swarm to issue, usually with the old queen, from the parent colony. Also called *primary swarm.*

**Propolis.** Glue-like, resinous materials collected from trees or plants by the bees and used to strengthen the comb, close up cracks, etc. Also called *bee glue.*

**Pupa.** The third stage in the development of an insect having complete metamorphosis. (The plural is *pupae.*) *See Larva.*

**Queen.** A fully developed, mated female honey bee. The queen is larger and longer than a worker bee.

**Queen cage.** A small cage in which a queen and five or six worker bees are confined for shipping and/or introduction into a colony.

**Queen cage candy.** Candy made by kneading powdered sugar with invert sugar syrup until it forms a stiff dough; it is used as bee food in queen cages.

**Queen cell.** A special, elongated cell, resembling a peanut shell in appearance, in which the queen is reared. It is usually an inch or more in length, and the inside diameter is about ⅓ inch. It hangs down vertically from the comb.

**Queen cup.** A cup-shaped cell that hangs vertically in a hive. It may become a queen cell if an egg is placed in it and if bees add wax to it. Natural queen cups, and most artificial ones, are made of beeswax, but plastic ones are also made.

**Queen excluder.** A device made of wire, or wood and wire, or zinc, having openings of about .163 to .167 inch that permit workers to pass through but exclude queens and drones. It is used to confine the queen to a specific part of the hive, usually the brood chamber.

**Queen substance.** This term usually refers to the complex of chemical substances secreted by at least three glands in a queen's body by which she is recognized. Queen substance serves to control social order.

**Requeening.** The replacement of one queen with another, usually older queen.

**Reversing.** The act of exchanging the positions of a colony's hive bodies, usually to encourage the upward expansion of a brood nest. Reversing may also break up the continuity of the brood nest to relieve congestion.

**Robbing or robber bees.** Bees that take honey from other colonies, or from exposed cappings, extracted supers or other sources. Robbing bees are usually aggressive, often fighting with other bees.

**Round comb honey sections.** Comb honey sections each containing about 7 or 8 ounces of honey when filled; these are patterned after Cobana sections.

**Royal jelly.** A highly nutritious glandular secretion of young bees fed to the queen and the young brood.

**Sex attractant.** A chemical substance that attracts an animal of the opposite sex of the same species for the purpose of mating.

**Shallow super.** A super of any one of several sizes that is shallower than a standard super. Commonly, shallow supers vary from 4¼ to 7 inches in depth.

**Solar wax extractor.** A glass-covered insulated box used to recover wax from combs and cappings by letting the heat of the sun melt it.

**Starter colony.** A usually queenless colony into which newly grafted worker larvae destined to become queens are placed for the first 24 hours of their larval life as queen cells. *See Finishing colony.*

**Super.** A hive body in which bees store surplus honey, so called because it is placed over or above the brood chamber.

**Supersedure.** The natural replacement, by a young queen, of the queen (her mother) in the hive. Shortly after the young queen commences to lay eggs, the old queen usually disappears (dies).

**Swarm.** The aggregate of worker bees, drones, and a queen that leaves the mother colony to establish a new colony. Swarming is the natural method of propagation of the honey bee colony.

**Thorax.** The central region of an insect's body, to which the wings and legs are attached.

**Tracheae.** The internal breathing tubes of an insect; the tracheae open into the spiracles at the body surface.

**Transition cell.** An irregularly shaped cell, usually smaller than a worker cell.

**Travel stain.** The darkened or stained surface of honey capped in the comb caused by bees walking on its surface and depositing traces of pollen or propolis.

**Uncapping knife.** A knife used to shave or remove the cappings from combs of sealed honey for extraction. The knives are usually heated by steam or electricity.

**Wax glands.** The eight glands of the honey bee that secrete beeswax. They are located in pairs on the last four visible ventral abdominal segments.

**Winter cluster.** The arrangement or organization of adult bees within the hive during the winter period.

**Worker bee.** A female bee whose reproductive organs are only partially developed. The worker bees carry out all the routine work of the colony.

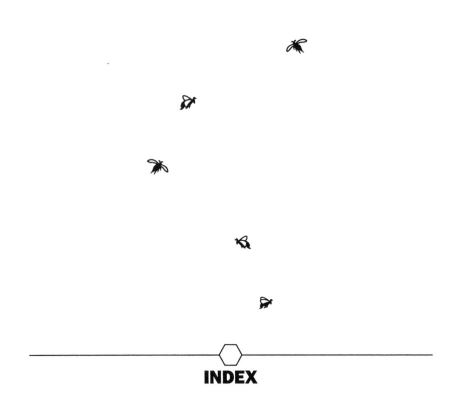

# INDEX

# How-to Books Available from The Countryman Press

## How-to and Nature Guides

*Backwoods Ethics: Environmental Issues for Hikers and Campers,* $13.00

*Backyard Livestock,* Revised Edition, $15.00

*Backyard Sugarin',* Third Edition, Revised and Expanded, $8.00

*Earth Ponds: The Country Pond Maker's Guide,* Revised and Expanded, $17.00

*Earthmagic: Finding and Using Medicinal Herbs,* $15.00

*The Earth Shall Blossom: Shaker Herbs and Gardening,* $18.95

*Fishwatching: Your Complete Guide to the Underwater World,* $18.00

*Our Native Fishes: The Aquarium Hobbyist's Guide to Observing, Collecting, and Keeping Them,* $14.95

*The New England Herb Gardener: Yankee Wisdom for North American Herb Growers and Users,* $15.00

*Perennials for the Backyard Gardener,* $18.00

*Sketching Outdoors in All Seasons,* $20.00

*Surveying Your Land: A Common-Sense Guide to Surveys, Deeds, and Title Searches,* $10.00

*Wilderness Ethics: Preserving the Sprit of Wildness,* $13.00

## Cookbooks

*The Best from Libby Hillman's Kitchen: Treasured Recipes from 50 Years of Cooking and Teaching,* $25.00

*Camp and Trail Cooking Techniques: A Treasury of Skills and Recipes for All Outdoor Chefs,* $20.00

*The King Arthur Flour 200th Anniversary Cookbook,* $21.00

*Seasoned with Grace: My Generation of Shaker Cooking,* $13.00

*Wild Game Cookery: The Hunter's Home Companion,* Revised and Expanded, $14.00

We offer many books on travel and outdoor recreation, as well as a selection of mystery novels. Our books are available through bookstores, or they may be ordered directly from the publisher. For shipping and handling costs, to order, or for a complete catalog, please contact: The Countryman Press, Inc., P.O. Box 175, Dept BK, Woodstock, VT 05091-0175; or call our toll-free number: (800) 245-4151.